Science in Veda

Science in Veda

Editor
D.R. Khanna

2009
DAYA PUBLISHING HOUSE
Delhi - 110 035

ISBN 81-7035-613-X
ISBN 978-81-7035-613-4

Published by : **Daya Publishing House**
1123/74, Deva Ram Park
Tri Nagar, Delhi - 110 035
Phone: 27383999
Fax: (011) 23260116
e-mail : dayabooks@vsnl.com
website : www.dayabooks.com

Showroom : 4760-61/23, Ansari Road, Darya Ganj,
New Delhi - 110 002
Phone: 23245578, 23244987

Laser Typesetting : **Classic Computer Services**
Delhi - 110 035

Printed at : **Chawla Offset Printers**
Delhi - 110 052

PRINTED IN INDIA

Preface

Blind faith in the Vedas has led the Hindus to consider them as an unlimited source of knowledge and even trace their authorship to God. In the last century, when discoveries and advancement of science began fast changing life patterns around the world, the reaction was varied. Some were for all out support to the scientists to go ahead, while others preached caution. And even as the controversy continued, the expanding horizons of science encouraged the spirit of competition and generally increased appetite for knowledge. Vedas are considered as an ocean of knowledge. Every bit of Vedas is very important each stanza, each line, each word has a significant meaning to it. For the language also supports its purpose. It is said that Sanskrit is the only nearest language which could be used to explain or describe anything clearly and specifically. It is the only Vedic Dharma where religion and Science go in hand to hand. The Vedas contain in them the gems of all true sciences.

The Book Science in Veda deals with the combined approaches of modern science and ancient Vedic science. As we know that Indian Scriptures and Sanskrit literature is the storehouse of knowledge. As we go through this literature they have innumerable illustrations of Science, technology, arts, music, dance, environment, architecture, vehicles etc. The present book is an attempt to explore the knowledge of science, penetrate the mystery of the Vedas and to search out in them the various branches of Science.

The Book Science in Veda is divided into ten chapters describing the importance of water as described in our vedic literature.

D.R. Khanna

Contents

Chapter 1

The Cosmological Code of Nasadiya Sukta in Rigveda

S.R. Verma*
Department of Physics,
D.B.S. (P.G.) College, Dehradun

Introduction

Recent scientific discoveries seem to validate the concept of Vedas. Physicists and Cosmologists are close to proving that science and Vedas seem to be saying the same thing. The purpose of this article is to explore the relationship between the concepts of Big Bang Theory of origin of universe and basic ideas in the Nasadiya Sukta of Rigveda. We shall see how the two foundation of twentieth century, Physics Quantum Theory and Theory of Relativity

*: Ex Principal, S.D. (P.G.) College, Hathras (U.P.)

both force us to see the world very much in the way Vedas and Upnishads see it. Creation is accompanied by the severest austerities–tapas of God. The word tapas also means heat. The whole universe was in a concentrated form which is mentioned as a point or bindu. The whole universe was in a single infinitesimal point, one single bindu, out of that explosion occurred. This theory is known as Big Bang theory. The seeds of Big Bang theory lie in Nasadiya Sukta of the Rigveda. Here it is shown that Nasadiya Sukta of Rigveda concurs with basic concepts of Big Bang theory of the origin of the Universe.

The question of the origin and evolution of the Universe fascinated mankind since long. Different civilizations, religions and cultures formulated their own interpretation.

There are some long standing questions about the Universe. Some of them are as follows:

1. Where did the universe come from?
2. How and why did it begin?
3. Will it come to an end and if so how?

These are questions that are of interest of all of us. In order to understand origin of universe scientists devise theories or models called cosmological models which gives descriptions of the universe that can be checked against observation. Most of the theories are based on general theory of relativity, quantum mechanics and gravitational law of attraction. There are basically two types of cosmological models:

1. Hot Big Bang Model
2. Steady State Model

The third one is Quasi Steady State Cosmology (QSSC) model which is modified form of steady state model. Jayant Vishnu Narlikar and his colleagues Fred Hoyle, Geoffrey Burbidge proposed this theory in 1993.

Discovery of microwave background radiation by A.A. Penzias and R.W. Wilson supports the Big Bang theory of origin of universe. The background radiation distributed throughout the universe was interpreted as a relic of Big Bang. The Big Bang theory based on Einstein's general theory of relativity was proposed by Alexander Fred Mann in 1922. According to Big Bang theory Universe began under extreme conditions approximately 15 billion years ago. The expansion of universe began on explosion of space at the beginning of time.

The biography of the Universe account for every thing in its nearly 15 billion years history except for an extremely small factors of second ($t < 10^{-43}$ sec) after Big Bang. As the universe cooled by expansion the unified field which was present at every close to the Big Bang beginning, subsequently unfold creating everything. As the universe expanded, both its temperature and density quickly dropped. This 'thinning out' and 'cooling' led to a series of practically instantaneous events highly significant for the present universe. Some of these were

1. Gravity breaks away from the unitary primeval force (unified force) as a separate entity, it happened shortly after 10^{-43} second and it soon become much weaker than other force.
2. The second of the four forces, the weak force breaks away and establish its own identity. Temperature dropping quickly and a little latter it is followed

by electromagnetic and the strong nuclear force. By the end of the hadron era [t = 10^{-43} sec to t = 10^{-4} sec. Temperature (°K) T = 10^{32} to T = 10^{13} and density $\rho = 10^{94}$ to $\rho = 10^{14}$ gm/cm^3] all forces have separated out and have changed significantly in strength.

3. Neutrinos decouple and begin to expand freely rather than being maintained in a thermal equilibrium with other constituents of the Universe. There should be a cosmic neutrino background as a result of this event.
4. Next, the decoupling matter and radiation makes the universe transparent to electromagnetic radiation detectable today as cosmic wave background. The universe has become radiation dominated.
5. The first atomic nuclei begin to form with the generation of helium in a ratio of about one helium nucleus to three hydrogen nuclei (protons). This is about the relative cosmic abundances of these two elements observed today.
6. With the energy density of the universe now low enough the electrons begin combining with nuclei to form stable atoms for the first time.
7. The essential constituents of the universe gave now all been established and it only remains for the matter to organize itself into the stars, galaxies and clusters of the galaxies.

This picture of Universe that started off very hot and cooled as it expanded is in agreement with all observation and evidence that we have today.

The Vedic seers had an intellectual urge to know how the Universe came into existence. How did the process start? What was the first principle or TATTVA that put the creative process into action. In fact there are several Sukta in Rigveda which provide us knowledge of force of gravitation, birth of star and origin of the universe. Among the various Suktas of Rigveda Nasadiya Sukta has been most popular among scholars. Nasadiya Sukta makes its own contribution to our understanding of the origin of the Universe.

Search Strategies

Many scholars of different countries esteem Vedic literature as it is the record of the ancient Indians' astronomical observations in disguise of the offerings to the gods who are none but the different celestial bodies or natural phenomena. The vedic seers realized that their profound knowledge would not be easily understood by common people and for this they represented the heavenly bodies etc. as gods and their motions as 'ratha' (Chariet) striding, etc. They stored their observational facts and the data of their research in verse in a cryptic language, as apparently these are nothing but the offerings to the gods.

To explore the cosmology and astronomy we have to depend on some procedures namely:

1. The hymns of vedas are interpreted by the finding the proper meanings of the words out of the possible meanings.
2. The inner meanings are unfolded through proper interpretations of the words.
3. The cryptic and metaphoric descriptions are deciphered.

4. The method of transcription by 'Katapayadi sutra' to the verse written in secret language is applied.

Meanings and interpretations of words used in this manuscript are based on Madhusudan Ojha's work entitled *'Desavada rahasya'* and A. Bhattacharya's work on ancient astronomical terms and their interpretation in the light of modern Astronomy, Calcutta. In our research work, we like to demonstrate how these methods can be made fruitful to Nasadiya Sukta in extracting advanced science and astronomy.

Results and Discussion

Nasadiya Sukta contains seven mantras:

Mantra 1

nāsadāsinno sadāsitta dā nim nāsidrajo
no vyomā paro yat |

Kimāvarivah Kuha Kasya Sarmannabhah
Kimasidgahanam gabhiram | |

[Rigveda Ch. 10, 129,1]

[The *rishi* says that there was neither *sat* nor *asat* at that time, *i.e.* at the time of the creation of the universe. There was no space, nothing else were present. Then what covered on? Where? The deep primordial waters also were not there at that time.]

At the time of the creation of universe the root cause which brings back the cosmic again cannot be named as 'asat' *i.e.* cannot be said to be non-existent because such thing cannot give rise to this universe. It cannot be called 'sat' also because nothing perceptible was present at that time. Actually author of the Nasadiya Sukta is going to say that 'sat' and 'asat' both existed together. He is going to uphold the concept of singularity at the time of Big Bang.

Singularity is the end of the road. Singularity is a place (or a point) where space and time simply disappear. At singularity normal concepts of space and time breakdown. Stephen Hawkings and Penrose went on to prove that not only could the universe begin in a singularity but that is actually it had begin in a singularity. This singularity that Stephen Hawkings and Penrose uncovered with their calculation is mathematically an event in space time where physical behaviour breaks down. You cannot figure out when and where something is going to happen if you do not have a clear background of time and space. We certainly cannot use science to tell us what existed before Big Bang. It shows that singularity was neither 'sat' or 'asat'. Then is not our sage scientifically correct.

The sage says that there were no (*vyoman*) space at that time. There was nothing to be covered or protected at that time and therefore no principle of envelopment existed. The word 'Kuha' means that there was no place to support to carry out the act of envelopment.

According to Big Bang theory universe was created under critical conditions. At the Big Bang itself is thought to have had zero size and so to have been infinitely hot. A very short time after the Big Bang space and time did exist in the way we think of them today. The Universe began as an infinitely dense cosmic singularity that expanded explosively in the event called Big Bang. It was not just matter that was created during the Big Bang. It was space and time were created. So in the sense that time has a beginning, space also has a beginning.

In this mantra says a poetic fashion by questioning what covered on? Where? By the first question he tells that some matter was created at some point. He is indicating toward the concept of Big Bang. This also shows that space was created which was covered by some matter. Big Bang theory agrees with this view.

The word 'Ambhas' usually means water. The root ambha means to sound. Hence *ambhas* should be taken as material producing sound. For that thing which originated in the space and which was very vast and unfathomable. The sage has coined a new word *ambhas*. Thus the word *ambhas* (sound producing matter) is scientific and appropriate. The sound that was created during Big Bang was the sound of *Om*.

In the first line if mantra the sage tells that there was nothing and in the next line he questions what covered on. Thus poetically he suggested that formation of *ambhas* took no time. Stephen Hawking, like most theoretical physicists now believes that the secret of the most elusive of all goals lie in the very early universe the period within the first trillionth of a second after the beginning of the Big Bang.

In the second line of Mantra the sage put the question "For whose shelter all this was prepared?" The sage did not know the answer so he has put forth his question to all the wise man. This question is still unanswered by the modern scientists.

Mantra 2

na mrtyurāsidamrtam na tarhi na ratryā
anha āsit praketah |

ānidavātam swadhaya tadekam tasmāddhanyanna
parah kimcanāsa ||

[Rigveda, Ch 10, 129, 2]

[The second mantra states that there was neither death, nor immortality. There was no indication of day or night. There was only that one breathing without air with its own energy. There was nothing else.]

The Seer's statement that there was only that one thing at the time of the birth of universe is accepted by all modern cosmologists. At the very instant of its creation, all matter and all four fundamental forces (gravitational force, electromagnetic force, nuclear force and weak interaction) were indistinguishable from each other. Sheldon Glashow, co-winner of the noble prize for his work with grand unified theories, once told, "When the universe was very, very hot, we believe that all the forces may have been one." That one underlying, seemingly magical force is what we are all now working to discover. According to Stephen Hawking when universe was about 10^{-43} of a second old, the four fundamental forces we see in our cold stable universe were probably one. As the universe expanded and cooled, matter and force split apart and then split again. It begins to suggest that there was a common origin for everything we see today in the Universe. It is presumed that gravity has just broken its bond with the single unified force that existed at the instant of the Big Bang at the wall of Plank time comes at 10^{-43} sec. We do not yet have a proper quantum theory of gravity which unifies with other fundamental forces.

In second mantra, the sage is indicating towards the single unified force at the very close to Big Bang. The physicists now realize that these division of fields (*i.e.* four fundamental forces like gravitation, electromagnetic, nuclear and weak forces) are nothing but different aspects of a single entity, the unified field.

The Rishi (*rsi*) says that there was only one primeval principle (Mula Tattva) which breathed without air for the sake of creation. The *prana* is only an outward indication of the fact that the entire cosmos to be created is already within this *Mula tattva*. During creation it only comes out just like air comes out from the lungs when we breathe out.

In this Mantra sage says that there was neither death nor immortality. This statement is true because there was no sun and no earth like there was no indication of day or night. This is also correct because unless there is a planet, rotating and travelling around a sun, there cannot be any day or night.

Mantra 3

tama āsittamasā gulhamgrepraketam salilam sarvamā idam |

tucchyenābhva hitam yadāsittapasas tanmahinā jayataikam | |

[Rigveda, Ch. 10, 129, 3]

[There was darkness to begin with, there was something mysterious in the darkness. It was impossible to understand. It was all undulating matter (*Salil*). *Abhu* originated from the surrounding was wrapped by lighter material. It developed further due to might of heat.]

The universe soon after its origin in the Big Bang passed rapidly through states of very high temperature from 1S–200S (approximately three minutes), when temperature of the universe dropped from 10^{10}K to 10^{7}K. At such high temperature free neutron and proton come together to form atomic nuclei. The time temperature relationship plays a significant role in early history of universe. The hydrogen atoms could not exist before 1 million years after big bang.

The background photons prior to t = 1 million years had energies greater enough to prevent electrons and protons from getting together to form hydrogen atoms. Only after t = 1 millions years have these photons been red shifted enough to permit hydrogen atoms to exist.

Prior to t = 1 million years, the universe was completely filled with a high energy photons colliding vigorously with protons and electrons. This state of matter is called plasma, and it is opaque. During the first million years of the universe, matter and energy formed an opaque flame. In this mantra *Rsi* has indicate towards this opaque by saying that there was something mysterious in darkness.

About 1 million years after the big bang expansion and red shift caused the temperature of the universe to fall below 3000 K so that protons and electrons could combine to form hydrogen atoms. Hydrogen is transparent so the universe suddenly became transparent. The transition from an opaque to a transparent universe occurred roughly 1 million years after the Big Bang. Once atoms had begun to form then matter could condense into galaxies and stars and gravity could start playing an important role in the development of the universe.

All this description is put in a nutshell of single word *'Salila'* by the sage. *'Salila'* means a matter with play of ripples or waves. *Salila* is the cosmic soup and not ordinary water.

The separate clouds or gas drops formed from the cosmic gas are represented by an appropriate word *'Abhu'*. *'Abhu'* means a thing formed from the surrounding material. *Abhu* originated from the surrounding was wrapped by lighter material. It develop further due to the might of heat.

Mantra 4

Kāmastadagre samavartatādhi manaso
retah prathaman yadāsit |

Sato bandhumasati niravindanhrdi pratisyā
kavayo manisā ||

[Rigveda, Ch. 10, 129, 4]

[The great worldly desire comes from the minute, invisible unworldly seed of mind in the same way *'Sat'* came from *'asat'*. The learned with far reaching intelligence have recognised this fact after complete thinking in the mind and through scanning in their hearts.]

In the first stage of creation there arose a desire in the mind of the almighty to create. The good deeds of being in the previous *kalpa* culminated in the form of a seed of the cosmos in the mind of the creator at the time of creation.

The learned after deep thought came to conclusion that all action associated with the observed cosmos have their origin in the discernible source. Now scientists start thinking that the facts of the Big Bang as they are slowly uncovered could suggest the work of a creator or creative force.

Science seems to have uncovered a set of laws that within the limits set by the uncertainty principle tells us how the universe will develop with time, if we know its state any time. The ultimate essence of the universe is space, consciousness is but a condition of space. The contents of the world is the distortion (*Vikara*) or desire of its container, consciousness space. The distorted 3-D space is *Sagun Brahma*. The space minus its *Vikara* or distortion (or desire) that is the unified field is *Nirgun Brahma*. *Brahman*–space is the ultimate reality underlying all existence.

Mantra 5

tiroscino vitato rasmiresāmadhah
svidasidupari svidasit |

retodhā āsanmahimana āsantsvadha
avastatpra yatih parastat ||

[Rigveda, Ch. 10, 129, 5]

The strands or rays scattered out were they oblique or downward or upward? They became germ holders and became mighty. Those who tried to keep themselves aloof remained small or those who surrendered themselves became inferior while those tried hard became superior.

The sage questions whether rays are oblique or downwards or upwards? By this question the sage indicates that there were no real directions in space such as upwards or downwards and oblique. The seer is also indicating the special features of the universe. The universe is homogenous and isotropic over large distance scale. In small scales universe in highly homogenous and an isotropic. The universe is expanding. The general theory of relativity and Big Bang theory are based on these special features of the universe.

The *rsi* further says that cosmic matter which was scattered in the space start gathering due to gravitational astronomical bodies of different size were formed. Some of these held themselves aloof so they remained small. These are names as *'Swadha'*. Some bodies surrounded themselves to others. These are also *'Swadha'*. Other bodies absorbed more and more matter and smaller bodies by gravitational attraction and became enormous. These are named as *Prayati.*

Our universe contains various galaxies of different shapes and sizes. It also contains number of quasars, supernova, Nebula, stars, white dwarf, neutron stars and black holes. The galaxies generally presumed to form from a primeval hydrogen gas cloud. The galaxies in addition to stars also contains large quantities of gas and dust and this material is constantly being converted into stars, planets, satellites and asteroids. The same concept is given by the sage using words *'Swadha'* and *'Prayati'*.

Mantra 6

ko addhā veda ka iha pra vocat kuta ājata
kuta iyam visrstih |

arvāgdevā asya visarjanenatha ko vedayata
ābabhuva ||

[Rigveda, Ch. 10, 129, 6]

[Who really knows? Who will be able to say from where this great universe came into being. The God is subsequent to the creation of the universe than who knows from what this universe originated?]

The Big Bang model provides a good frame work for understanding the early evolution and present structure of the universe. Many questions and ambiguities and neither addressed nor answered within the concept of the Big Bang model. For example it leaves a number of questions unanswered.

1. Why did the Big Bang occur?
2. Why was the early universe so hot?
3. Why, how and when did matter first appear in the universe?

4. Why is the universe so homogenous and isotropic over large distance scale?

The more we fine tune our outer vision and probe deeper into eternal questions, our limitation in relation to the vastness and mysterious of space become more apparent. Whether we see the cosmos through our mind's eye or through telescopic eye the enigma that is cosmos only gets deeper. This quality of a eternal mystery of the cosmos is brought out in 6th mantra of Nasadiya Sukta of Rigveda. In this mantra Rishi says it is very difficult for any body to say exactly how all that we see around us came into being. He says that he is well aware of the complexity of the problem.

Mantra 7

iyam visrstiryata ābabhuva yadi vadadhe
yadi vā na |
yo asyadhyaksah parame vyomanso cna
veda yadi vā na veda ||

[Rigveda, Ch. 10, 129, 7]

[Who knows whether this universe is supported by the creator or not? Does he who is the highest authority of the universe and who is in the super space know it definitely or not?]

The sage tells here that universe is supported by its creator. Here sage suggest that probably that superior power knows how the universe is created and then he raised suspicion whether this is the final authority or is there anyone else superior still. Expressions of such doubts are very common among vedic seers. They were earnest seekers of truth.

The science has pointed very clearly in the direction of the Big Bang creation of the universe, but the cause of the Big Bang still remains very much enigma. The philosophers have often concluded that there must be a 'first uncaused cause' and this they have identified with God. The Big Bang theory of the beginning of the universe seems at first sight to satisfy their proof. Scientific explanations comes to an end, provided a God gives opportunity to ascribe the universe to a transcendent cause. A cosmologist can say nothing about transcendent causes.

Thus we can see that whatever cosmologist with all their ultra modern equipments say today about the origin and fate of the universe their seeds are already present in *Nā Sadiya Sukta* of Rigveda.

Conclusion

In conclusion we must say that there are two basic attempts in studying the vedas apart from the religious or philosophical aspects. First one is the usual tradition which is effort in finding some scientific facts regarding origin of Universe and birth of stars only at optimum level from the vedas to establish that these facts were discovered long before the western people were able to discover them. These researches should be encouraged as they contribute towards the history of science and astronomy.

The other aspects of the studies started from the belief of the people that the Vedas are the complete Science or Vijnana in the real sense containing both the *para* and *apara* knowledge. The belief has tempted the researchers to decipher the knowledge of various kinds from the vedas by applying different methods. Of course, these methods may or may not be the right keys in extracting the knowledge from the vedas, but these must be considered, to be basic steps towards finding the right key for proper utilization of treasure in the vedas.

References

Das, A.C., 1971. *Rigvedic India,* 3rd Revised edn., New Delhi.

Hawking, Stephen W., 2001. *Universe in Nutshell.* Bantam Press, U.K.

Holay, P.V. *Vedic Astronomy.* Published by Shri Baba Saheb Apte Smarak Samitee, Apte Bhawan, Nagpur.

Kaufmann, William J., 1985. *Universe.* W.H. Freeman and Company.

Sarasvati, S.P. and Vidyalankara, 1987. *Rigveda Samhita.* Veda Pratishthana, Delhi.

Sastry, T.S. Kuppanna, 1985. *Vedanga Jyotisa of Lagadha.* Indian Science Academy, New Delhi.

Sen, U., 1974. *The Rigvedic Era,* Calcutta.

Tilak, B.G., 1956. *The Arctic Home in the Vedas,* Poona.

Tilak, D.G., 1893. *The Orion.* Tilak Brothers.

Wilde, S., *et al.,* 2001. *Nature,* 209: 175–178.

Chapter 2
Rain Making by Yajna

P.P. Pathak
Department of Physics,
Gurukul Kangri University, Haridwar

ABSTRACT

This chapter gives scientific analysis of possible changes in environmental conditions due to yajna (specifically performed for rain making) that may lead to rain.

Introduction

This is another scientific procedure given in Vedas. Ritual of yajna specifically performed for the purpose of rain making is clearly better then modern scientific method of artificial rain making by cloud seeding with silver iodide or dry ice (CO_2) from aircraft, because of being very expansive as well as uncertain in success. Simultaneously it also brings down the seeded material along with rainwater. This material may be harmful to the crops etc. Success of this modern method depends on the presence of super cooled water in the clouds. Thus the presence of clouds becomes prerequisite for artificial rain making by seeding. Also premature release of precipitation often destroys updraughts and causes dissipation of clouds decreasing overall rainfall. Thus, under extreme draught condition, when generally clouds are not present, rain making by seeding method is not possible.

As the different chapters of this book describe the vedic methods for different purposes, this chapter describes and analyses the yajna for rain-making.

Yajna for Rain Making

General procedure for yajna is to burn wooden pieces (called samidha) inside a conical shaped pit or vessel with a square shaped upper open end as of variable sizes. A mixture of many materials (called samagri) is poured along with ghee on this fire along chanting of vedic hymns (different for different purposes). For example, daily yajna for general well being is performed in a small vessel of square end of about 20–30 cm and of similar depth.. This is done for about 15 minutes. But the yajna for rain making is performed on large scale in open space for many hours and for many days because the aim is to change the atmospheric conditions. Therefore a pit of a meter square conically going down, is made in the ground.

Materials and Method

The main differences in yajnas for different purposes lie in materials (samidhas and samagri) and methods (mainly Mantras and duration of aahuties). There is variation in these materials as used by different vedic pundits. The author of this chapter talked personally to three pundits at different times and contacted one more with letter. Some time in 1987, I talked to Mr. Vishwa Bandhu Shashtri (then president of D.P. Arya Pratinidhi Sabha) who told detailed list of samagri and samidha as given in Table 2.1. Along with this 50 per cent green wood of bamboo and Karir other 50 per cent drywood of papal may be used.

Table 2.1: Substance with their Quantities to be Used as Samagri

Sl.No.	*Substance (Hindi Name)*	*English and Botanical Name*	*Quantity*
1.	Nagarmotha	Nut grass (*Cyperus scariosus* R. Br.)	40 kg
2.	Makhana	Lotus seed roasted (*Nelumbo nucifera and Euryale ferox*)	20 kg
3.	Vaybidang		10 kg
4.	Tulsi-dal and beej	Tulsi leaves and seeds (*Ocimum sanctum*)	4–5 kg
5.	Gola	Coconut (*Cocos nucifera*)	4 kg
6.	Peela chandan	Yellow sandalwood	3–4 kg
7.	Sarson	Mustard (*Brassica campestris*)	3 kg
8.	Guglu	Indian bdellium (*Commiphora mukul*)	2.5 kg
9.	Chirongi	Chirongi (*Buchanania lanzan*)	2 kg
10.	Shatavari	Shatavar (*Asparagus racemosus*)	2 kg
11.	Chandan	Sandalwood (*Santalum olbum*)	2 kg
12.	Lal Chandan	Sandalwood red (*Pterocarpus santalinus*)	2 kg
13.	Khand	Raw sugar	2 kg

Contd...

Table 2.1–Contd...

Sl.No.	Substance (Hindi Name)	English and Botanical Name	Quantity
14.	Devdaru	Cedar (*Cedrus deodara*)	2 kg
15.	Giloy	Heart leaved moon-seed (*Tinospora cordifolia* Miers)	1.5 kg
16.	Nirmaliphal		1.0 kg
17.	Dalchini	Cinnamon bark (*Cinnamomum tamala* Nees)	1.0 kg
18.	Tagar	Tagar (*Valeriana wallichiana*)	1.0 kg
19.	Badi ilayachi	Cardamom	1.0 kg
20.	Javitri		1.0 kg
21.	Jayphal		1.0 kg
22.	Vacha	Vacha (*Acorus calmus*)	1.0 kg
23.	Ghee		1.0 kg
24.	Taleeshpatra	Talpatra (*Curculigo orchioides*	0.5 kg
25.	Jatamasi	Jatamasi (*Nardostachys grandiflora*)	0.5 kg
26.	Munakka	Dry grapes (*Vitis vinifera*)	0.5 kg
27.	Kapoor	Camphor (*Cinnamum camphora*)	0.25 kg
28.	Kesar	Saffron crocus (*Crocus sativous* 1)	50–60 gm

Another Pandit (Late) Mr. Hari Prasad Sharma (a Retired Principal, Gurukul Mahavidyalaya, Jwalapur) was contacted some times in first quarter of 1988. He did not reveal the details of materials etc. The third pundit contacted by letter was (Late) Mr. Virsen Vedshrami (of Ved Sadan, Indore). He sent his book written by him about this procedure. Another book by Swami Vidyanand "Videh" published by ved sansthan Ajmer also gives the details of the procedure. Samagri given by this book is shown in Table 2.2.

Table 2.2: Statistics of Success in Rain Making by (Late) Mr. V.B. Shastri

Place	*No. of Times*	*Result*	*Remarks*
Dharur (Maharastra)	Once	Rain with thunder	Clouds were formed within few hours of yajna and heavy rain observed within 9–12 hrs.
Bidar (Karnataka)	Seven	Rain with thunder	
Hingoli (Maharastra)	Once	Rain with thunder	
Raichur (Karnataka)	Once	Rain with thunder	
Gwalior (M.P.)	Once	Rain with thunder for 4–5 days continuously	
Daha (U.P.)	Once	Did not rain	

Possible Changes in Atmosphere Due to Yajna

The whole process of yajna as described in section 2 above is carried out in open atmosphere. The continuous fire for hours together, increases the temperature and ionization in surrounding air. Burning of green wood releases water vapour into the air, which increases humidity. Burning of many materials listed in the Tables 2.1 and 2.2 produces many types of aerosols particles and pouring of ghee (a kind of animals oil made by heating and melting butter and then filtering) releases its vapours along with aerosol which make their surface oily. Thus yajna produces following changes in the atmosphere:

1. Increase in air temperature.
2. Increase in water vapour content.
3. Increase in ionization.
4. Increase in aerosol number density; surface of aerosols is oily.

Table 2.3: Statistics of Success of Rain Making by (Late) Mr. H.P. Sharma

Time of Year	*Place*	*Result*	*Remarks*
Jan. 79	Gurukula Vrindavan (U.P)	Clouds formed and rained	No details of thunder were provided
May 79	–do–	Rained heavily for three days	
June 79	Mathura (U.P.)	Rained for an hour	
Aug. 79	Vrindavan (U.P.)	Cloud formed remained for 5 hours but dissipated without rain.	
Sept. 79	Etah (U.P.)	Rained for half an hour	
Sept. 79	Muzaffarnagar (U.P.)	Cloud formed remained for 5 hours but dissipated without rain.	
Feb. 80	Vrindavan (U.P.)	Cloud formed, no rain	
Sept. 81	Khaira (Mathura, U.P)	Rained heavily for two hours	
Sept. 82	–do–	Cloud formed, rained very little	
Jan. 82	Kharaut (Mathura, U.P.)	Rained for 4 hrs.	
Oct. 82	Silani (Haryana)	Cloud formed remain for 4 hours, rained very little.	

All these changes influence the production of rain in following ways:

Influence of Increase in Temperature and Humidity

Increase in the air temperature and humidity produces instability in atmosphere. Buoyant air parcels start rising from above the fire. As the process is continued for many hours, a large number of air parcels go on rising. These air parcels with large amount of water vapour become saturated soon after rising above the ground and condensation starts to form cloud cells. It is worth mentioning here that depending on the humidity present in ambient air, the rising air parcels are diluted by entrainment of relatively dry air. This process of dilution however, is reduced after some time when more and more water vapours are released to increase humidity in surrounding air. Thus large convective clouds may be formed within the duration of yajna or after that when the fire is continued in yajna kunda by putting dry and green wooden pieces, by all people present.

Influence of Ionization

Ionization in the air produced by fire is expected to play important role in formation of rain in two ways:

1. Because of this large ionization, the cloud parcels are expected to be charged and are helpful in nucleation. Famous work of Wilson (1899) showed vapour could condense on ions. Further, Varshneya (1971), Chan and Mohnen (1980) and Singh *et al.* (1985) have shown theoretically that the presence of ions enhances the nucleation rate and thus the nucleation on charged aerosols is faster than that on uncharged particles. Therefore, the nucleation would start on ions and charged aerosols and very soon large drops would be formed. In upper parts of clouds where subzero temperatures are found and the water may exist in super cooled state, presence of ions helps in deposition of super cooled tiny water droplets in forms of snow as observed in laboratory experiments by Varshneya (1969). As the

temperature at lower level is higher, these snow particles come down in form of raindrops.

2. According to the experimental results of Vonnegut *et al.,* (1962) the cloud cell developed from the region of high ionization show more electrical activity probably because of more electrification through convective mechanism (Vonnegut 1955). In a relatively recent study Israelson *et al.* (1986) also concluded that increase in ionization due to radioactive fallouts enhanced thunderstorm activity in Sweden. Thus one may conclude that high ionization at lower levels of atmosphere enhances the electrification of the clouds developed. And electrified clouds are expected to give more rains, after lightning (Moore, 1977).

Influence of Aerosols

Because of burning of many materials listed in Tables 2.1 and 2.2 many types of aerosols (mainly coke particles of different types) are expected to be carried with rising air parcels. Properties of these aerosols are not known. Some of these may be hygroscopic. Also the vapours of ghee make their surface oily. Both the hygroscopic nuclei and the nuclei with oily surface would enhance nucleation rate. Thus the increase in aerosol number density also enhances the possibility of rain.

The above explanations may account for the observed success in rain making. It is worthwhile to compare this ancient Vedic method of rain making with modern scientific method of artificial rain making by seeding experiments. As mentioned in introduction above, presence of cloud is prerequisite and presence of super cooled water in them is necessary for the success of seeding experiments for rain making. But the vedic method does not require any condition. It changes humidity; forms cloud by creating unstability in atmosphere and provide means for fast nucleation and rain. The presence of high humidity and/or clouds would be helpful of course, and time of getting rain would be reduced, but it is not necessary and the method can give rain even in complete dry conditions. Only the duration of yajna needed would be enhanced. As regards to expanses, the vedic method is very economical as compared to seeding experiments. Total expenditure in one attempt comes to about Rs. 4000/. (About US$ 300/-), while a seeding experiment would cost many times more.

Conclusion

The above theoretical analysis of the possible changes in the atmosphere due to a rain making yajna, it becomes evident that it is quite possible to make rain by this Vedic method. Also it seems that this Vedic method of artificial rain is better and economical than the modern scientific methods presently in use. This is evident from the fact that it also helps in formation of clouds even in dry weather conditions by increasing humidity and creating unstability by adding hot water vapours into atmosphere in huge quantities. The experimental testing of properties of aerosols being released and verification of electrical (ionized) state of rising air remains to be carried out which may further strengthen the view of possibility of rain.

Acknowledgement

Thanks are due to (Late) Mr. Vishwa Bandhu Shastri, former Head of U.P Pratinidhi Sabha, for providing the list of materials, statistics of success (in Tables 2.1 and 2.3) and detailed method for performing yajna. Thanks are also due to (Late) Mr. H.P. Sharma, former president of Vristi Vigyan Mandal, Mathura and (Late) Mr. Virsen Vedsharami of Ved Sadan Indore for their statistics of success in rain making yajna. Thanks are also due to Mr. Satyavrat Rajesh former professor in Ved department, G.K.V. for many fruitful discussions on the topic. Most of English and Botanical names (in Table 2.1) are provided by Dr. P. Kaushik, Department of Botany. Help and cooperation of Mrs. Manju Pathak (my Wife) in finding some of these is greatly appreciated.

References

Barry, R.G. and Chorley, R.J., 1976. *Atmosphere, Weather and Climate*. Methuen and Company Ltd., p. 109.

Chan, L.Y. and Mohnen, V.A., 1980. Ion nucleation theory. *J. Atmos. Sci.*, 37: 2327–2337.

Israelson, S., Schutte, T., Pisler, E. and Lundquist, S., 1987. Increased occurrence of lightning flashes in Sweden during 1986. *J. Geophys. Res.*, 92: 10996–10998.

Moore, C.B., 1977. An assessment of thunderstorm electrifications. In: *Electrical Processes in Atmospheres*, (Eds.) H. Dolezalek and R. Reiter. Dr. D.S. Verlag, Darmstadt, pp. 333–352.

Singh, N., Rai, J. and Varshneya, N.C., 1985. The effect of ions on cloud condensation and ice nucleation. *Am. Geophys.*, 3.

Vonnegut, B., 1955. Possible mechanism for the formation of thunderstorm electricity. In: Proc. *Conf. Atmospheric Elec. Portsmouth, Portsmouth N.H., Geophys. Res. Pap.* 42, AFCR-TR-55-222, 169–181.

Vonnegut, B., Moore, C.B., Segmonin, R.G., Bullock, J.W., Staggs D.W. and Bradley, W.E., 1962. Effect of atmospheric space charge on initial electrification of cumulus clouds. *J. Geophys. Res.*, 67: 3909–3922.

Varshneya N.C., 1971. Theory of radiation detection through supercooled liquid. *Nucl. Instruments and Methods*, 92: 147–150.

Wilson, C.T.R., 1899. On the comparative efficiency as condensation nuclei of positively and negatively charged ions. *Phil. Trans. Roy. Soc.*, 193(A): 289–308.

Chapter 3

Concepts of Yajna and its Impact

Sudha Dubey
Department of Zoology,
Holkar Science College,
Indore – 452 001, M.P.

Introduction

Scientific Aspects of *Yajna*

There are two basic energy systems in the physical world: Heat and Sound. In performing yajna, these two energies, the heat from yajna's fire and the sound of the Gayatri and other mantras, are combined to achieve the desired physical, psychological and spiritual benefits.

The fumigation of specific substances in the *Yajna*–fire is a scientific method of sub-utilisation of matter into energy and expanding its power and positive effects in the surrounding atmosphere. The electromagnetic waves generated thereby also help in transmitting, at cosmic level, the desired sonic signals "stored" in the mantras, which are chanted during the process of sacrificing the special material preparations in the fire.

Chanting of Sanskrit Mantras

The power of sound vibrations is long since acknowledged in the field of science because these vibrations can penetrate the energy spheres at the subtle and cosmic levels. All the alphabets of the Sanskrit language are endowed with special vibrational powers, which set out harmonious wave patterns when pronounced.

It is interesting to note that Dr. Howard Steingull, an American Scientist has established that recitation of Gayatri Mantra produces 110,000 sound waves per second. In fact recitation of the Gayatri mantra during the fire worship (yajna) act as a complementary to each other. The patterns of chanting of the mantras are so designed that they latently contain the essence of the music or the quintessential sound of the torrent of life sustaining energies emanating from the cosmic energy center of the corresponding mantras. (The cosmic energy center associated with the Gayatri mantra is Sun). Uttering of these mantras produces vibrations which are soothing to human mind and all plant and animal life. These vibrations also help in spreading specific energy waves in the surrounding atmosphere as the oblations are offered.

Purification of Environment by *Yajna*

The industrial complexes, rapid urbanization, deforestation, air and water pollution, disturbance in the ozone-formation, radioactive wastes etc., have destabilized the human, animal and plant life cycles. The ecological imbalance caused by these acts of 'civilized men' has resulted into disastrous threat not only to the human survival but to the life as a whole on our planet.

Till recently it was accepted that research into science can give answer to nearly all of man's problems. Today we find increasing number of diseases including malfunctioning of body organs due to the increasing severity of pollution in the atmosphere. Ozone depletion has been causing ailments like sunburn, skin cancer cataracts and weakening of the immune system. Viruses are becoming drug–resistant and showing consistent growth trends.

Experimental studies show that the incidence of physical ailments, sickness and disease becomes less in the houses where the yajna (*agnihotra*) is regularly performed because it creates a pure, nutritional and medicinal atmosphere. It renews the brain cells, it revitalizes the skin, and it purifies blood and prevents growth of pathogenic bacteria.

Agnihotra is basically a healing process. 'Heal the atmosphere and the healed atmosphere will heal you'–is the modes operandi [5].

Purification of environment through the constituent electrons of the substances fumigated in the *Yajna* is an obvious side-effect of this process [2–4]. The observations of some distinguished scientists are noteworthy in this regard.

Dr. Hafkine has mentioned that–"Mixing ghee and sugar and burning them creates smoke which kills the germs of certain diseases and secretion takes place from some glands related to the wind-pipe which fills our heart and mind with pleasure."

"Burning sugar and its smoke have great power to purify the atmosphere. It kills the germs of T.B., measles, smallpox and cowpox"–remarks *Prof. Tilward.*

According to *Dr. Shirowich,* a Russian scientist of the recent times–"After successful experiments, we have collected the following data about the cow and yajna which even the people of India do not know:

1. Cow's milk contains the great power of protection from atomic radiation.
2. Houses having cow dung–covered floors enjoy complete protection from atomic radiation.
3. If cow's ghee is put into fire, its smoke will lessen the effect of atomic radiation to a great extent. This process is known as yajna in Indian languages."

The medicinal fumes emanating from the process of *agnihotra* have been observed by researcher in the field of microbiology to be clearly bacteriostatic in nature, which eradicate bacteria and micro-organisms which are the root causes of illness and diseases. This must be the reason why the incidence less in the households where *agnihotra* is regularly performed.

Even without going detailed chemical bacteriology, it can be stated that performance of yajna leads to purification of air. This takes place in the following four ways [2]:

Removal of Foul Odors

As already stated, under steam volatalisation, the various volatile oils get diffused in the surrounding atmosphere along with steam and smoke. Since these oils have distinct good smell, the foul odors are automatically replaced. This aroma can be experienced easily in the surrounding when yajna is performed and is due to diffusion of substances like thynol, eugenol, piene, terpinol and oils of sandlewood, camphor and clove.

Removal of Bacteria

As stated under products of combustion, the partial oxidation of hydrocarbons and decomposition of complex organic substances produce formaldehyde which is a powerful antiseptic. It is also interesting to note that germicidal action of formaldehyde is only effective in the presence of water vapours which is also produced in large quantities in yajna. The use of formaldehyde spray for disinfecting of walls, ceiling etc., is common and such a spray is automatically produced when yajna is performed.

The oxidation of hydrocarbons also produces formic acid and acetic acid both of which are good disinfectants. Use of formic acid in preserving vinegar is a common knowledge.

The antiseptic and antibiotic effects of smoke of yajna have also been examined by conducting suitable experiments on rabbits and mice and it has been established that smoke emitted in yajna is a powerful antibiotic.

Agnihotra ash purifies and cleanses the water making it fit for drinking [5].

Removal of Insects

There are non-bacterial parasites like flies, ringworm, dice fleas etc., which are normally difficult to deal with since bactericides which can be used against them are also harmful to other living beings. Such insects are generally immune to ordinary reagents. However they either get killed or are driven away when they come in contact with volatile oils like camphor which are diffused in the environment.

Effects on Plants and Vegetation

The disinfection of air is not only useful to animal life but it also helps plants' life through the bacteria responsible for diseases in both may be different. The aromatic substances which get diffused in the air offer protection to plant life against distinctive organisms. This ensures a healthy plant growth. Agnihotra's atmosphere and ash can be used as adjustants in the 'Natural Farming' methods– also known as the agnihotra farming methods. It is a holistic concept of growing plants in pure and healthy atmosphere and balancing the ecological cycles by performing agnihotra (yajna) in the middle of the farm and using the yajna–ash as a fertilizer. It is not only safe and productive but also holistic in its approach towards environment.

Role of CO_2 Generated in Yajna

The wood and fossil burning in atmosphere is always controversial because of generation of CO and CO_2 and increase in consequent 'green house' effect. On similar lines it can be argued that performance of yajna also produces CO and CO_2. It should be noted here that the way in which the samidhas are burnt in yajna is a process of slow combustion. It is not comparable with the burning of coal in factories or for household fire or running of machineries etc., where oxygen is sucked in large quantities and CO_2 is emitted in huge quantities. In the slow combustion taking place in the process of yajna, no large quantity of O_2 is utilized nor CO_2 is emitted in such a quantity that poses any burden to the environment. In fact whatever CO_2 is generated is readily absorbed by the surrounding plant life and vegetation and CO_2 cycle is strengthened [4].

The other important aspects are the fact that CO_2 produced in yajna is not free CO_2 but it is mixed with other aromatic oils and antiseptic products. It also acts as a vehicle in transporting such products to the surroundings.

The use of CO_2 as a cerebral stimulant to assist the patients suffering from lack of ventilation is common in medical world. Its use to control and cure many mental disorders is also known to medical science. Small amounts of CO_2 inhaled by the persons performing yajna acts as a stimulant and more and more aromatic fumes are inhaled which helps curing of mental disorders.

Particularly effective results with respect to the elimination or reduction in radiation were achieved through yajna's fire and ash. These observations are made by Dr. L. Matela Anatoninhowska of Poland after using P.S.I. techniques.

The conception of gyana and vigyana seem to have changed today. Today's gyana is confined to intellectual acquisition through visible fact or otherwise perceivable experiences. Laboratory instruments and methods based on concurrent logic and established theories of modern science are governing the domains of the vigyana today.

The scientific research and technological development are interwoven and both are based on use of matter in one form or the other from nano-particles to Gagantic structures or extraction, transformation and exploitation of energy through material media. But this approach is highly expensive. Moreover, it largely demands excessive use of natural resources and is not always ecofriendly. The discoveries and inventions of erdite scientists and professors have made enormous contribution to the advancement of the scientific knowledge and its technological applications in the physical domains of life. But this kind of knowledge does not help elevation of virtues, human values or generation of generous sentiments, altrustic attitude, etc. Hence this kind of knowledge however advance it may be, does not contribute to gyana. On the contrary, the scientific and technological advancement has to a great extent added to people excessively comfort driven and artificial life and thus, through indirectly whetted their selfish, extravagant, arrogant, pompous attitudes and cunning cleverness.

Now if we look in term of vigyana, then also we find its achievement mired in its controversies, lacunae and setbacks and also its negative impact on the quality of life. Scientific progress or technological innovation in one direction produces obstruction or hazardous risks in the other. For instance, use of chemical fertilizers does increase agriculture production in the short run, but the crops produced thereby contains several chemicals that are harmful to health: also the use of synthesized chemicals gradually diminishes the fertility of the soil. Technological advancement and the associated industrial growth have no doubt gifted us with the excellent accessories ranging from ultra fast communication, transportation facilities, medical diagnostic tools and treatment, luxurious living standards and what not–but the fact that they have, in more than one ways, polluted and toxicated air, water and natural environment of life up to an alarming level is also very well known to all of us. The excessive consumption of natural resources has posed threats of another kind.

Savants, including frontline scientists, have expressed global concerns due to the most likely exhaustion of natural resources of fuel like coal, crude oil, petrol, etc. What will happen to our vehicle and rapid movements then? Electricity can't be a substitute because already there is scarcity in its production and supply in most parts of the world. Dwindling water resources have already annulled hydro energy based production of electricity. Moreover, the use of nuclear energy beyond the safer limits, risks the deadly threat of radio activity. In other words, the unilateral progress of science in the modern age has been contrary to what vigyana is supposed to be.

The roots of gyana and vigyana in the vedic times were very different from today. Both the streams today have emanated from and remained confined to, the gross manifestation and materialistic existence of nature. The studies, experiments, invention and growth of gyana and vigyana in the Rishi age had evolved from the realisation of the sublime world of consciousness force. In simple terms, the foundational basis today is materialism were as that of vedic age its was spirituality. Modern science has now recognized that whatever is perceivable in gross domains of nature is negligible as compared to what exist in the subtle, invisible, extra sensory expansion. For example, the existence of million gallon of water in some part of the earth indicates the presence of several billion times larger amounts of water in the form of vapours or subtler particles in the sky every where.

Modern science has also accepted the ancient concept that mental determination and thoughts are also sources of energy, which can be used to generate 'magnet'–like force of attraction. Further it also needs a asserting that the sublime and invisible world of nature might be the genesis and controllers of its gross manifestation. The vedic rishis had realized this scientific fact and therefore choosen sublime realms of nature as the basis of their research.

They found that a miniature universe, both in terms of atomic and subtler particles and sublime energies of nature is present in the human body and mind. They devised specific sadhna procedures and practises to awaken the hidden potential and unlimited energies in their own bodies and minds. This spiritual approach to vigyana also enabled them to extract and use at will, the material powers and vital energies in cosmos as well. Most remarkable was the fact that their awakened inner self had always inspired and altruistic and sane application of vigyana in total harmony with nature. Their gyana was attained by a scientific approach to spirituality.

Ultimate enlightenment through the spiritual sadhnas of gayatri mantra and altruistic experiments of yagya were the paramount source of their inner awakening and enlightened acuman and consequent comprehensive approach and ideal accomplishment in gyana and vigyana.

"Gayatri" and "yagya " and therefore revered as the divine parents of vedic culture. Gayatri is the eternal mother of gyana and yagya is the origin of vigyana. The meaning and implications of each of the 24 words of the gayatri mantra encompasses the knowledge to inspire and guide an aspirant on the noble path to self awakening and universal well being. The sonics structure of each of its syllables and the collective configuration in the great mantra is unique and most powerful according to the subtle science of sabda Brahm.

As experienced and expounded by the great vedic Rishis and the saint and demonstrated in the lives of sages and spiritual yogis of the later times as well, the japa-sadhanas of Gayatri mantra, if practiced as per yagya is performed. Several successful experiments on agnihotra (yagya) have been reported in recent times in these respects. Therapeutic healing and growth of vital energy and vigor of those who regularly participate in suitable yagyas for such effects for prescribed periods of time have been authentically verified in some scientific laboratories, too.

The power-currents generated by performance of yagya are also said to have elevating effect on the mental and emotional states of the participants and on the sublime ambience. This is perhaps the reason why yagya is regarded so sacred and is performed in every important Hindu-religious ceremony and on the occasion of religious festivals. It also happens to be an integral part of each of the sixteen vedic sacraments performed at significant transitional stages of life from prenatal stages till death. The akhand agni lighted at the time of birth as per hindu customs is yagya symbolizing the continuity of life; funeral after death is also performed as a yagya in which the gross body, the gift of nature, is sacrificed in the form of fire to return it in its basic constituents (the pancha tatvas) to the nature. Yagya is thus the key to the grand vigyana of well being and auspicious welfare and the progress of the gross physical, materialistic and the emotional spheres of life and healthy sustenance of nature.

From our highest good, we need to retrieve the global approach to gyana and vigyana in order to revive the divine culture on the earth. The divine inspiration and the powers gayatri and yagya Sadhnas would enable us to accomplish this and usher into the new bright era of global peace, prosperity and happiness.

Notes

1. Sadhna devout spiritual endeavors with ascetic disciplines; self refinement and self transformation through self determination and efforts.
2. Siddhis supernatural potentials and miraculous attainment.
3. Sabda brahmin the omnipresent perpetual vibration or sublime sound generated by the eternal of cosmic consciousness.
4. Japa repeated rythmic enunciation with meditation.

Chapter 4
Glimpses of Physics in Vedic Hymns

B.P. Shukla
Retired H.O.D., Department of Physics,
Gurukula Kangri University, Hardwar – 249 404

Any serious scholar of modern science have gone into the depth of his subject and engaged in research activity, soon comes to realise that modern science is incapable of answering several intricate questions regarding the creation of universe and the ultimate reality of nature. The mind of a true seeker of reality gets perturbed by looking at various theories coming up during the course of development of sciences which provide only partial explanation of any phenomenon. I have also been confronted with such a situation. At this stage I was reminded of Vedas. There is a famous book written by Roman poet Lucretius in the form of verse named 'De Rerum Natura'–meaning 'On the Nature of things'. This is in seven volumes and its translation is available in several languages. This book is pregnant with several scientific thoughts. It is said that quit a number of scientific discoveries of the present era owe their origin to this book. This could become possible only because the great Scientists of west focussed their attention on this text. It is also claimed that this book shall be the source of several new discoveries for the scientists of future. Needless to emphasise that India is highly rich in her cultural, scientific and spiritual heritage. Vedas are the oldest written document in the history of humanity.

Vedas have attracted the attention of the noted scholars of east as well as those of west. Huge commentaries on *Vedic Samhitas* have been written by the scholars of different ages.

The very foundation of the Gurukul Kangri Vishwavidhayalaya was laid on the authenticity of Vedas for study of *vedic* literature along with modern sciences and literature. It is, therefore, quite natural to the study Vedas in the light of modern sciences. Keeping this in view a course of "Physics and Vedic Thought" was introduced at the postgraduate level in physics right from the time of its inception in 1991. Since then this course is being taught to the students of M.Sc. Physics. This has been greatly appreciated by the students and the academic community.

The course includes some chosen verses from different Vedas, *viz., Rigveda, Yajurveda* and *Atharvaveda.* First of all the literal meaning of verses is explained and then the scientific interpretation is given. It is found that the interpretations truly confirm the findings of modern physics. This is not all, some of the Vedic verses make declaration of scientific theories, which need research and verification. It is also an astonishing fact that several verses mention about facts and theories, which were discovered at a much later date, *e.g.*, gravitation and heliocentric structure of solar system.

However, it has been most unfortunate that Vedas did not attract the attention of scientific community. Most of Vedic commentaries have been written by the scholars of humanities and theology. The natural consequence is that the cardinal scientific facts within Vedas have hardly been brought to lime light, what to talk of putting them to experimental test.

This article is primarily and exclusively devoted to bring forth the fact of Vedic Samhitas which contain any kind of thought pertaining to Physics.

The word Veda own its origin to Sanskrit root vid- meaning knowledge. So knowledge of almost every field is found in Vedas in an integrated form. Unlike the tradition in modern times, it is not categorised, as Physics, Chemistry, Maths, Economics, Sociology, Philosophy. Hence the scholars of any discipline can enter into the study of Vedas and they shall be wonder struck to see that almost all of these disciplines are revealed in Vedic verses.

In spite of all this, there are people, with an air of scholarly ostentation, who consider it as an exercise in futility to search the sciences in Vedas. To such prejudiced scholars I would suggest to contemplate on the following assertion made by Swami Vivekanand in his–Paper on Hinduism, 19th September 1893 presented in the Parliament of Religion, Chicago.

The Vedant philosophy, at which the latest discoveries of science seem like echoes".

This assertion has not been made by an ordinary mortal but by an ascetic who had completely realized, God and soul. Hence, this cannot be anything but truth.

I have been hearing about Vedas right from my childhood from my revered father and others of elder generation. I was also found of attending religious congregations organized by different sect of Hindus including Arya Samaj.

In all these congregations I found one thing in common authensity all of them sublimity without exception, stressed upon the Vedas. This infused in a curiosity about Vedas. It was the destiny of my fate that after passing my M.Sc. in Physics. I got an opportunity to serve Gurukul Kangri Vishwavidyalaya, as a Lecturer of Physics. Needless to mention that this Vishwavidyalaya was founded by late Swami Shraddhanand Ji Maharaj (a prominent disciple of Swami Dayananad Saraswati–the founder of Arya Samaj) with a view to impart Vedic education alongwith the study of modern subjects. Here I got ample opportunity to listen to and interact with various learned scholars of vedic literature, to name, few of them Pt. Priyavrat Vedvachaspati, Pt. Satyavrat Siddhantalankar, Pt. Buddha Dev Vidyalankar (who acquired the name Swami Samarpananandji after taking renunciation Sanyes). Pt. Buddhadeo Vidyalankar persuiaded me to enter upon scientific interpretation of Vedas. He specially pointed out to me some hymns from Yajurved for this purpose. Perhaps the time was not ripe. Hence, I could not proceed. It was only in the year 1991 when P.G. classes were started in

Physics that I could manage to introduce a course "Physics and Vedic thoughts" in the syllabus of M.Sc. Physics. The response has been quite encouraging and now a research programme in Vedic Physics is being Organised. We now focus our attention on some Vecid samhitas and analyse their content is the light of Physics.

Sprituo-Materialistic Concept

Modern Physics is purely materialistic in its approach in probing into the secrets of nature and for that purpose its study is mainly focused on matter and energy. However, the glimpses of Physics found in Vedas go far beyond this limit. In dealing with the phenomena of Universe. Vedas take into consideration two more entities in addition to matter and energy. These are the individual soul and the Universal Soul. The phenomena of the Universe cannot be understood only on materialistic basis. The Universe is spirituo-materialistic. The Universe is governed by Eternal Law and nothing can escape its authority. This is revealed in the following hymns.

Rig. 1. 64–44

There are three luminous entities which are responsible for the performance of various operations of the Universe in accordance with law and order. One of them (Divine Spirit) sows the seed in the beginning of creation cycle of the world, the other one (soul) observes the world by all its powers and the third one is matter, whose forces are perceived in active manifested forms but its essence cannot be comprehended easily.

Thus it is seen that Vedic thought takes into consideration two conscious entities (God and Soul) in addition to matter. It is worthwhile to mention here that, in the modern era, when the frontiers of Physics are reaching their climax, a suggestion has been made by a noted Physicist Prof A.S. Eddington to add the element of free will in elementary particles. He has come to this conclusion on the basis of a deeper analysis of Heisenberg's uncertainty principle. If elementary particles have free with then they must have consciousness as well which supports the Vedic view regarding conscious entities governing. Another salient point mentioned in the above verse is the complexity of matter. This view also finds its full support from modern physics in which fantastic efforts have been made to explore the structure of matter. What to talk electron, proton and neutron and hundreds, of elementary particles discovered so far including guarks, the mystery of matter has not been resolved. It has been predicted that quarks have also an structure and particles constituting them have been predicted and named as pre quarks.

Matter, Energy and Origin of Universe

We now take a look on some Vedic verses which give a description of matter, energy, forces of nature and origin of Universe.

Rig. (10–72–4)

The earth ows it originated to sun and the directions have been prescribed with respect to earth. The primordial matter "Aditi" (which was in the unmanifest form) became manifest with the help of energy. The manifest matter acquired different forms and names due to association with energy and energy got different names due to its association with matter.

Reg. (10–90–16)

The manifested world has come into formation by the elements of nature (Akas, Vayu, Agni, Apah, and Prithivi) by Virtue of forces of integration and disintegration. These forces of nature were present in the primeval state of matter. The elements of nature combined with energy and dissolved in space, where the elements and forces of nature of previous cycle were dissolved.

Reg. (10–130–1)

As a consequence of integration and disintegration the world is stretched out with the various threads of material substances and is further extended by the hundreds of elemental actions and reactions. It is woven like a textile piece by the protective powers of nature, which pervade everywhere. When the world is extended these powers continue to maintain the strength of its warp and weft.

Reg. (10–82–6)

At the time when the creation began to take place atoms of material substances caught the all creating spirit in their embryo wherein all natural forces got submerged. In the naval of eternal matter there was one supreme spirit which is responsible for the sustenance of all the worlds.

It is worthwhile to mention that a similar assertion has been made by the famous Physicist Sir Isaac Newton "God made this world and gave it a momentum" this statement is a curious mixture of science and religion.

Atharva (11–1–1)

The heat which pervades all over the world become active at the time when "aditi", the materia radica (primordial matter) cooks the mess of cosmic creation for progrinition under Divine control. The seven physical elements (Dravya, Guna, Samavaya, Abhava, Karma, Visesa, Samavaya) which are the cause of manifested objects, with all their effects and forms churn out this heat.

Commentary

The verses cited above, give a very clear description of matter and energy. According to Vedic view energy is the property of matter and it can not exist without matter. The terms "aditi" "deva", "pitarah", and "Riashayah" etc. are used for matter, material elements and for energy as well as.

"Aditi" is primordial matter when it is in the state of equilibrium, the role of energy is not perceptible. But even in this state energy is present in the matter.

According to Vedic darshan (philosophy) there are five elements these are Akas (ether), Vayu (air), Agni (fire), Apah (water), and Prithivi (earth). These elements exist in their finer state called "Suksma Bhuta". The modifications of these elements are found in the gross form known as "Sthula Bhuta" they are also known as "Bhuta and mahabuta" respectively. Infact energy is the property of these elements. The term "Bhuta" means matter combined with energy. A detailed account regarding this is found in "Sankhya" and Vaisesika" system of Indian philosophy–which have their origin from Vedas.

An account of these subject is found in several Vedic verses.

Rig (10–45–1)

First of all the fire was born in solar region in the form

of the sun. In next step it appeared in the terrestrial objects as Jatvedas and finally it took its place in the atmosphere as "Nrimanah" in the form of electricity which is the benefactor of creatures. One, who understands the properties of fire greatly appreciates it and makes use of it in several ways.

Rig. (2–1–1)

The electricity is generated from the rays of Sun, it is generated from water, it is generated from stones (lode stone) it is produced from wood as well as from herbs. It is the source of protection for human beings and may cause destruction as well as it creates light.

The truth of the revelations made in the above mentioned Vedic hymn is verified by the fact that in modern times electricity is being generated by almost all the sources mentioned above, the most prominent among these are solar, electricity and hydro electricity.

The Universe

The universe has been discussed in Vedas in a great detail. We find the description regarding galaxies, stars, solar system, earth and gravity in vedic hymns. The details given in Vedas are verifiable and are found to be amazingly accurate. As an example a few verses are cited here.

Reg. (1–164–1, 10–27–15)

The above cited verses mention that only seven planets of our solar system (from Mercury to Saturn) originated from Sun while the rest three (Uranus, Neptune and Pluto) were captured by the Sun form outside by its strong gravitational field.

Rig. (1–164–5, 1–140–5)

In these verses it has been revealed that seven planets were born in a series of explosions, after the explosions these were in the gaseous form and they slowly condensed to become solid planets.

Rig. (1–164–6)

Out of the seven planets emanating from sun only six condensed to become full planets where as the seventh condensed into small pieces and has been termed as unborn planet. Thus the above cited verse assets the definite truth about the belt of asteroids found between planets Mars and Jupiter.

Some scientists of our time have conjectured that a planet was broken in to pieces on account of some catestrophy giving rise to the belt of asteroids found between Mars and Jupiter. However, the truth revealed in the Vedas is just opposite.

Rig. (10–149–1)

The Sun has sustained the earth and establized the heavenly region in the space by virtue of its gravitational powers. The Sun makes the clouds tremble like a horse in the agitated atmosphere and churns out the ocean placed in the atmosphere region.

It this verse it has been made clear how the solar system is maintained which includes our earth. It also throws light on the atmospheric electricity and rains.

Rig. (1–164–2)

A single wheeled chariot of the sun is yoked to seven rays which make out one white ray and this white ray draws the chariot. The wheel of the chariot is comprised of three navels dividing the chariot wheel into three sectors denoting summer, rainy and winter seasons which come one after the other during the period of its complete rotation *i.e.* year (samvatsara). This rotation is imperishable and irresistible where in rest all the worlds.

Chapter 5
Yagya Therapy for Tuberculosis

Navneet[1], Prabhat[1], Reeta[1] and Dinesh Chandra[2]
[1]Department of Botany and Microbiology,
[2]Department of Ved,
Gurukul Kangri University, Hardwar

Tuberculosis has affected mankind from very ancient times. Records on the tablets of Babylo-Assyrians, writings of the Hindus, Chinese and Mesopotamians, skeletal remains of tuberculosis lesions from the Iron age, Peruvian and Egyptian mummified human remains from the time before Christ have amply proved the prevalence of this disease since antiquity. The disease associated with cough, fever, blood spitting and emaciation, and recognized as Laoping (lung cough, lung fever) in China and Rajayakshma (king among diseases, Kshaya-tissue getting withered) in India, was called Phthisis (Phthinein, to waste away) by Hippocrates (460–377BC). Johann Schonlein in 1839 named this disease as tuberculosis (tubercula, a small lump, T.B).

Nature of the Disease

The early Greek physicians like Aristotle, Aretaeus, and Galen thought that the disease was transmissible through contagion, Varro (1160–28 BC) thought that the disease might be caused by organisms which could not be seen by human eyes. Paracelsus, Frascatorius, Benjamin, Marten and Budd believed that consumption might be caused by minute living creatures (*Contagium vivum*). Jean Villeman (1827–1892) established the contagiousness of tuberculosis and thought that the disease was caused by "ta morbid germ capable of multiplication". The German physician Robert Koch on 24 March, 1882 in Berlin announced that tuberculous affections of man and animals are caused by tiny slender, rod shaped bacilli and called them as tubercle bacilli (*Mycobacterium tuberculosis*).

Epidemiology

Tuberculosis is an ubiquitous infectious disease known to have existed from ancient times. The disease has been perpetuated and maintained in the human population since then. The incidence and mortality were high when the disease affected susceptible groups, as they offered favourable conditions for the spread of the disease. This is evident from the fact that the poor housing, poor sanitation, overcrowding, poor nutrition, overwork and stressful conditions of life in the cities lowered people's natural resistance to infection, making them an easy prey for the development of tuberculosis. Tuberculosis was relatively uncommon in India in the first half of the nineteenth century. There was a gradual increase in the mid-nineteenth century and the peak in tuberculosis incidence towards the end of the nineteenth century. The epidemiological study carried out in old Delhi from 1962 to 1991 showed no decline in sputum positive case rates from 3.3 per 1000 over 30 years period. There was a decrease in prevalence of radiologically active and probably active abacillary pulmonary tuberculosis from 13.2 per 1000 in 1962 to 5.4 per 1000 in 1991. The tuberculosis mortality has now shown on annual decrease due to the improvement in the standards of living and the introduction of on effective chemotherapy, which reduced the number of infectious active cases.

The Mycobacteria

The causative organism of tuberculosis is *Mycobacterium tuberculosis.* The generic name Mycobacterium (the name is derived from its mould-like growth pattern) was proposed by Lehman and Newman in 1896. *M. tuberculosis* is an aerobic thin, rod shaped, straight or slightly curved organism, of 1–4 microns length and 0.3–0.6 microns breadth, with rounded ends. It occurs singly or occasionally in clumps. The organism is non-motile and has no capsule. Mycobacteria can exist in mammalian (human and bovine), avian (*M. avium*) and piscine (*M. marinum*) forms. *Mycobacterium tuberculosis var hominis* is the organism concerned with the production of tuberculosis in man.

Infection and Host

M. tuberculosis must enter the body to produce infection and disease. The host tissue react to the infection and may effectively control it by mounting an immune response, by producing cell-mediated immunity (CMI) and delayed type tissue hypersensitivity (DTH). The infection occurs by inhalation of airborne droplet nuclei containing tubercle bacilli. The bacilli discharged from a pulmonary focus are brought out by the patient during coughing, spitting, talking, shouting, singing and sneezing as droplets. These infected, tiny droplets of mucus get dried and become droplet nuclei. They remain suspended in the air. Transmission usually requires close, frequent or prolonged exposure. Though exposure to tubercle bacilli is necessary for initiation of an infection but its progression into a disease depends upon genetic, immunological, environmental, physiological and of other factors like diabetes mellitus, H.I.V. infection and AIDS.

Pathogenesis

Tuberculosis is a chronic intracellular infection and the disease has a complex pathogenesis. Tuberculosis infection occurs in the form of primary tuberculosis and non-primary tuberculosis. The primary tuberculosis develops after the first infection with *M. tuberculosis*. The organisms gain entry into the lungs by way of inhalation of airborne droplets containing the infectious agent and are deposited. A primary lesion develops in the site of infection *i.e.* in the middle to lower zones of the lung, draining lymphatics of the area, and regional lymphnodes-branchopul monary and tracheobronchial regions. Primary tuberculosis is common in childhood and adolescence.

Non-primary tuberculosis refers to all forms of tuberculosis that occur after the first few weeks of primary tuberculosis. Non-primary tuberculosis can develop from both endogenous reactivation and exogenous reinfection. Endogenous reactivation (recrudescence of the initial infection) results from tubercle bacilli acquired by initial tuberculosis which remained viable but dormant in the tubercles in a lymphnode or in the lung. These bacilli are capable of exhibiting metabolism and replication if there is lowering of local immunity and flareup of an old infection. The natural resistance of the host is lowered by factors like age, concomitant disease, hormonal changes and immunosuppression. Exogenous reinfection develops with virulent tubercle bacilli in individuals who had primary infection many years earlier. Though primary tuberculosis occurs in any part of the lungs, the bacilli must reach the apical region for progression of infection to disease.

Chemotherapy

The introduction of chemotherapeutic regimens has revolutionised the treatment of tuberculosis. In pre-chemotherapy era *i.e.* before 1945, the treatment was towards strengthening of the patient's resistance to the disease. The measures taken were the avoidance of physical and mental strain, prolonged bed rest in a sanatorium, good food, fresh air and collapse therapy. Chemotherapy is antimicrobial treatment. It is capable of elimination of bacilli from the sputum, heal the lesions and cause their sterilization. The effect of chemotherapy depends upon biological, environmental and pharmacological factors. The drugs have the capability to kill fully viable organisms-exhibiting metabolic activity and continuous multiplication. The bacterial population contains heterogeneous bacterial group, some organisms are dormant most of time and exhibit growth during a short period. These are called as persisters and are not affected by most drugs. The chemotherapeutic agents vary in their capability to enter into all tissues and cells, moreover, the pH and the oxygen tension play an important role in influencing the antimicrobial effect of the drug. *Tubercle bacilli* survive best in an environment with a PO_2 of 100 to 140 mm Hg, 5 per cent CO_2 and a pH of 7.40. Streptomycin exhibits its activity in a slightly alkaline environment whereas pyrazinamide acts largely in an acid medium. The dose of the drugs must produce an inhibitory concentration in the sites of the bacilli. For example, the peak serum level attained is important for the response of the drug. Hence, isoniazid is given once a day in a dose of 300mg instead of divided doses. The treatment regimen against tuberculosis should contain a combination of two or more drugs. The chances of the emergence of resistant organisms is greater with monotherapy so a combination of drugs is used in the treatment. It has an advantage of preventing the multiplication of a small population exhibiting resistance to one drug. The antituberculosis drugs should have bactericidal activity, sterlizing action, to prevent the emergence of acquired resistance and the ability for intermittent use.

Failure of Chemotherapy

Though every tuberculosis patient has an excellent chance of being cured with chemotherapy but success rate with routine treatment is low (50 per cent). This high rate of failure is due to the treatment with inadequate regimens, irregular intake of drugs, frequent interruptions, the patient's early discontinuation of drug intake, insufficient duration of treatment, adverse reaction to drugs (intolerance hypersensitivity and toxicity) and initial drug resistance.

Thus there is multiplication of non-susceptible mutants and the emergence of drug resistance strains from such a therapy. In order to tackle this problem the patient has to be motivated at the start of treatment to perform yajna regularly along with the drugs.

Yajna Samagri for Tuberculosis

The diagnosis of pulmonary tuberculosis at an early stage of its development helps in the institution of effective therapy and enhances the likelihood of its success. The medicines prescribed to the patient depends upon the symptoms and the condition of the patient in different pathies like allopathy, homeopathy etc. Similarly in yajna therapy the constituents of yajna samagri varied according to the condition of the patient. The tuberculosis patients are classified into four categories on the basis of the clinical features and manifestations of the disease (Agnihotri, 1949). The symptoms of various categories are given below:

Stage 0

In this category the persons are included with no clinical symptoms but are likelihood of exposure to tuberculosis. The body structure of some persons are like that of an infected patient *e.g.* narrow chest, bend in backbone, cheeks inside. The other group includes those who are in contact with the patients suffering from tuberculosis *e.g.* doctors, nurses, relatives etc. They should use the yajna samagri ment for normal persons and perform yajna daily.

Stage 1

The patient may feel depressed and become tired at the end of the day and this feeling becomes more prominent and he may become easily tired during the day and after normal activity. In the beginning the cough is mild and dry especially in the morning and occurs in the form of clearing the throat. There is little pain in the chest after the meals which moves up to shoulders and back. The discomfort in the chest increases in case of pleurisy. There prevails the problem of indigestion and patient does not like ghee and other fatty materials. Moreover, there is increase in heart beat and the patient feels some problem during breathing. The hoarseness of voice is noted in some cases. Patient often complains of fever in the evening.

Stage 2

There is loss of appetite. The cough is persistent during night and sometimes it is associated with mucoid expectoration and blood tinged sputum may be present. The patient feels difficulty during breathing and wasting of the body leads to weakness. Palpitation of heart is noticed. In the acute tuberculosis the fever may be persistent throughout the day or subside and reappear intermittently. In the morning when fever subside it is followed by profuse sweating. There is some reddishness on the cheeks of the patient.

Stage 3

There is acceleration of all the symptoms described above. In this stage the cavities are formed inside the lungs. The cough is persistent and more frequent in the morning and is associated with mucoid expectoration. The bleeding from a tuberculous lesion varies from blood tinged sputum to a large amount of bright red blood. Sometimes the bleeding is profuse and is due to flooding of bronchial tree. The fever is high in the night and in the morning it subside

Table 5.1: Yajna Samagri for Tuberculosis

Sl.No.	Common Name	Botanical Name	Family	Part Used	Stage 0	Stage 1	Stage 2	Stage 3
1.	Guggul	*Commiphora mukul*	Burseraceae	Gum	+	+	+	+
2.	Chandan (White)	*Santalum album*	Santalaceae	Wood	+	+	+	+
3.	Chandan (Red)	*Pterocarpus santalinus*	Leguminosae	Wood	+	–	+	+
4.	Agar	*Aquilaria agallocha*	Thymelaeaceae	Wood	+	+	+	+
5.	Tagar	*Valeriana wallichi*	Valerianaceae	Root	+	+	+	+
6.	Chirounji	*Bachanania lanzan*	Anacardiaceae	Flower	+	+	+	+
7.	Coconut	*Cocos nucifera*	Palmae	Fruit	+	–	+	+
8.	Jaiphal	*Myristica fragrans*	Myristicaceae	Seeds	+	+	+	+
9.	Laung	*Eugenia caryophyllata*	Myrtaceae	Fruit	+	+	+	+
10.	Munakka	*Vitis vinifera*	Vitaceae	Fruit	+	+	+	+
11.	Kesmish	*Vitis vinifera*	Vitaceae	Fruit	+	+	+	+
12.	Ilaychi (bari)	*Amomum aromaticum*	Cannaceae	Fruit	+	+	+	+
13.	Rose	*Rosa indica*	Rosaceae	Flower	+	+	–	+
14.	Harad	*Terminalia chebula*	Combretaceae	Fruit	+	+	+	+
15.	Rice	*Oryza sativa*	Gramineae	Fruit	+	+	+	–
16.	Kapur	*Cinnamomum camphora*	Lauraceae	Stem (Gum)	+	+	+	+
17.	Sugar	*Saccharum album*	Gramineae	Stem	+	+	+	–

Contd...

Table 5.1–Contd...

Sl.No.	Common Name	Botanical Name	Family	Part Used	Stage 0	Stage 1	Stage 2	Stage 3
18.	Chuhara	*Phoenix sylvestris*	Palmae	Fruit	+	–	+	+
19.	Gilogy	*Tinospora cordifolia*	Menispermaceae	Whole Plant	+	+	+	+
20.	Brahmi	*Centella asiatica*	Umbelliferae	Whole Plant	–	+	+	+
21.	Indrayan	*Cirullus colocynthis*	Cocurbitaceae	Fruit	–	+	+	+
22.	Shalparni	*Desmodium gangeticum*	Fabaceae	Whole Plant	–	+	+	+
23.	Makoi	*Zizyphus oenoplia*	Rhamnaceae	Whole Plant	–	+	–	+
24.	Rasana	*Pluchea lanceolata*	Compositae	Leaves	–	+	–	+
25.	Jatamansi	*Nordostachys jatamansi*	Valerianaceae	Root	–	+	–	+
26.	Pandri	*Randia uliginosa*	Rubiaceae	Whole Plant	–	+	–	–
27.	Gokhru	*Tribulus terrestris*	Zygophyllaceae	Fruit	–	+	–	+
28.	Amla	*Emblica offcinalis*	Euphorbiacae	Fruit	–	+	–	+
29.	Jivanti	*Leptademia reticulata*	Asdepiadaceae	Stem	–	+	–	+
30.	Punarnava	*Boerhavia diffusa*	Nyctaginaceae	Stem	–	+	–	+
31	Choor	*Pinus roxburghi*	Pinaceae	Stem	–	+	+	+
32.	Khoobkalan	*Sisymbrium irio*	Cruciferae	Seed	–	+	–	+
33.	Jaun	*Hordeum vulgare*	Gramineae	Fruit	–	+	+	+

Contd...

Table 5.1—Contd...

Sl.No.	*Common Name*	*Botanical Name*	*Family*	*Part Used*	*Stage 0*	*Stage 1*	*Stage 2*	*Stage 3*
34.	Til	*Sesamum indicum*	Pedaliaceae	Seed	–	+	+	+
35.	Shatavar	*Asparagus racemosus*	Liliaceae	Root	–	+	+	+
36.	Adusa (bisauta)	*Adhatada vasica*	Acanthaceae	Whole Plant	–	+	+	+
37.	Almond	*Prunus amygdahus*	Rosaceae	Seed	–	+	+	+
38.	Keshar	*Crocus safivus*	Iridaceae	Flower	–	+	+	+
39.	Kapur Kachree	*Hedychium spicatium*	Zingiberaceae	Root	–	–	+	+
40.	Kut	*Saussurea lappa*	Compositae	Root	–	–	+	+
41.	Kulanjan	*Alpinia galanga*	Zingiberaceae	Rhizome	–	–	+	+
42.	Javitlri	*Myristica fragrans*	Myristicacae	Flower	–	–	+	+
43.	Devdar	*Cedrus deodaru*	Pinacacae	Wood	–	–	+	+
44.	Khas	*Vetiveria zizaniodis*	Graminae	Root	–	–	+	+
45.	Howber	*Juniperus commnunis*	Pinaceae	Fruit	–	–	–	+
46.	Nagar motha	*Cyperus rotundus*	Cyperaceae	Stem	–	–	–	+
47.	Honey							
48.	Seasonal Fruits							
49.	Halwa							
50.	Kheer							
51.	Cow Ghee							

but due to profuse sweating the patients clothes become wet. The loss of weight and falling of hairs is common. Loss of appetite, indigestion and loose motions makes the patient lean and thin.

क्षय

तासु त्वान्तर्जरस्या दधामि प्र यक्ष्म एतु निर्ऋतिः पराचैः।
एवाहं त्वां क्षेत्रियान्निर्ऋत्या जामिशंसाद् द्रुहो मुच्चामि वरूणस्य पाशात्।
अनागसं ब्रह्मणा त्वा कृणोमि शिवे ते द्यावापृथिवी उभे स्ताम् 2:10:5

प्र विशतं प्राणापानावनड्वाहाविव व्रजम्।
व्यन्ये यन्तु मृत्यवो यानाहुरितरान् छतम्।। 3:11:5

उत्तमो नाम कुष्ठास्युत्तमो नाम ते पिता।
यक्ष्मं च सवन नाशय तक्मानं चारसं कृधि।। 5:4:9

मा स्मैतान्त्सखीन् कुरूथा बलासं कासमुद्युगम्।
मा स्मातोऽर्वाडैः पुनस्तत् त्वा तक्मन्नुप ब्रुवे।। 5:22:11

इयमन्तर्वदति जिव्हा बद्धा पनिष्पदा।
तत्वा यक्ष्मं निरवोचं शतं रोपीश्च तक्मनः।। 5:30:16

निर्बलासं बलासिनः क्षिणोमि मुष्करं यथा।
छिनद्ध्यस्य बन्धनं मूलमुर्वार्वा इव।। 6:14:2

विद्रधस्य बलासस्य लोहितस्य वनस्पते।
विसल्पकस्योषधे मोच्छिषः पिशिंत चन।। 6:127:1

यः कीकसाः प्रशृणाति तलीद्यमवतिष्ठति।
निर्हास्तं सर्वं जायान्यं यः कश्च ककुदि श्रितः।। 7:80:3

पक्षी जायान्यः पतति स आ विशाति पुरूषम्।
तदक्षितस्य भेषजमुभयोः सुक्षतस्य च।। 7:80:4

विद्म वै ते जायन्य जानं यतो जायान्य जायसे।
कथं ह तत्र त्वं हनो यस्य कृण्मो हविर्गृहे।। 7:80:5

यं देवा अंशुमाप्याययन्ति यमक्षितम मक्षिता. भक्षयन्ति।
तेनास्मानिन्द्रो वरूणो बृहस्पतिरा प्याययन्तु भुवनस्य गोपाः।। 7:86:6

व्यावात् ते ज्योतिरभूदप त्वत्तमो अक्रमीत्।
अप त्वन्मृत्युं निर्ऋतिमप यक्ष्मं नि दध्मसि।। 8:1:21

यस्य तक्मा कासिका हेतिरकमश्वस्येव वृषणः क्रन्द एति।
अभिपूर्वं निर्णयते नमो अस्त्वस्मै।। 11:2:22

यदस्या गोपतौ सत्या लोम ध्वाङ्क्षो अजीहिडत्।
ततः कुमारा म्रियन्त यक्ष्मो विन्दत्यनाम नात्।। 12:4:8

सर्वज्यानिःकर्णो वरीवर्जयन्ती राजयक्ष्मो मेहन्ती 12:5:22

वरणो वारयाता अयं देवो वनस्पतिः।
यक्ष्मो यो अस्मिन्नाविप्दस्तमु देवा अवीवरन्।। 10:3:5

नडमा रोह न ते अत्र लोक इदं सीसं भागधेयं त एहि।
यो गोषु यक्ष्मः पुरूषेषु यक्ष्मस्तेन त्वं साकमधराङ्. परेहि।। 12:2:1

अघशंसदुः शंसाभ्यां करेणानुकरेण च।
यक्ष्मं च सर्वं तेनेतो मृत्यं च निरजामसि।। 12:2:2

संकसुको विकसुको निर्ऋथे यश्च निस्वरः।
ते ते यक्ष्मं सवेदसो दूराद् दूरमनीनशन्।। 12:2:14

ये यक्ष्मोसो अर्भका महान्तो ये च शब्दिनः।
सर्वान् दुर्णामहा मणिः शतवारो अनीनशत्।। 19:36:3

न तं यक्ष्मा अरून्धते नैन शपथो अश्नुते।
यं भेषजस्य गुल्गुलोः सुरभिर्गन्धो अश्नुते।। 19:38:1

ग्रीवाभ्यस्त उष्णिहाभ्यः कीकसाभ्यो अनूक्यात्।
यक्ष्मं दोषण्यमंसाभ्यां बाहुभ्यां वि वृहामि ते।। 20:96:18

ऊरूभयां ते अष्ठीवद्भ्यां पार्ष्णिभ्या प्रपदाभ्याम्।
यक्ष्मं भसद्य श्रोणिभ्यां भासदं भंससो वि वृहामि ते।। 20:96:21

यक्ष्मा

अक्षीश्यां ते नासिकाभ्यां कर्णाभ्यां छुबुकादधि।
यक्ष्मं शीर्षण्यं मस्तिष्काज्जिव्हाया वि वृहामि ते।। 2:33:1

ग्रीवाभ्यस्त उष्णिहाभ्यः कीकसाभ्यो अनूक्यात्।
यक्ष्मं दोषण्यमंसाभ्यां बाहुभ्यां वि वृहामि ते।। 2:33:2

हृदयात् ते परि क्लोम्नो हलीक्ष्णात् पार्श्वाभ्याम्।
यक्ष्मं मतस्नाभ्यां प्लीह्नो यक्नस्ते वि वृहामसि।। 2:33:3

आन्त्रेभ्यस्ते गुदाभ्यो वनिष्ठोरूदरादधि।
यक्ष्मं कुक्षिभ्यां प्लाशेर्नाभ्या वि वृहामि ते।। 2:33:4

ऊरूभ्यां ते अष्ठीवद्भ्यां पार्ष्णिभ्यां प्रपदाभ्याम्।
यक्ष्मं भसद्यं श्रोणिभ्यां भासदं भंससो वि वृहामि ते।। 2:33:5

अस्थिभ्यस्ते मज्जभ्यः स्नावभ्यो धमनिभ्यः।
यक्ष्मं पाणिभ्यामग्ङु. लिभ्यो नखेभ्यो वि वृहामि ते।। 2:33:6

अग्ङे. अग्ङे. लोम्निलोम्नि यस्ते पर्वणिपर्वणि।
यक्ष्मं तवचस्यं ते वयं कश्यपस्य वीबर्हेण विष्वच्चं वि वृहामसि।। 2:33:7

मुच्चामि त्वा हविषा जीवनाय कमज्ञातयक्ष्मादुत राजयक्ष्मात्।
ग्राहिर्जग्राह यद्येतदेनं तस्या इन्द्राग्नी प्र मुमुक्तमेनम्।। 3:33:1

व्यार्त्या पवमानो वि शक्रः पापकृत्यया
व्यहं सर्वेण पाप्मना वि यक्ष्मेण समायुषा।। 3:31:2

वि ग्राम्याः पशव आरण्यैर्व्यापस्तृष्णयासरन्।
व्यहं सर्वेण पाप्मना वि यक्ष्मेण समायुषा।। 3:31:3

त्वष्टा दुहित्रे वहतुं युनक्तीतीदं विश्वं भुवनं वि याति।
व्यहं सर्वेण पाप्मना वि यक्ष्मेण समायुषा।। 3:31:5

अग्निः प्राणान्त्सं दधाति चन्द्रः प्राणेन संहितः।
व्यहं सर्वेण पाप्मना वि यक्ष्मेण समायुषा।। 3:31:6

प्राणेन विश्वतोवीर्यं देवाः सूर्यं समैरयन्।
व्यहं सर्वेण पाप्मना वि यक्ष्मेण समायुषा।। 3:31:7

आयुष्मतामायुष्कृतां प्राणेन जीव मा मृथाः।
व्यहं सर्वेण पाप्मना वि यक्ष्मेण समायुषा।। 3:31:8

प्राणेन प्रणतां प्राणेहैव भव मा मृथाः।
व्यहं सर्वेण पाप्मना वि यक्ष्मेण समायुषा।। 3:31:9

उदायुषा समायुषोदोषधीनां रसेन।
व्यहं सर्वेण पाप्मना वि यक्ष्मेण समायुषा।। 3:31:10

आ पर्जन्यस्य वृष्ट्योदस्थामामृता वयम्।
व्यहं सर्वेण पाप्मना वि यक्ष्मेण समायुषा।। 3:31:11

मा बिभेर्न मरिष्यसि जर द्रष्टिं कृणोमि त्वा
निरवोचमहं यक्ष्ममेग्ड.भ्यो अग्ड. ज्वरं तव।। 5:30:8

अग्ड. भेदो अग्ड. ज्वरो यश्व ते ह्रदयामयः।
यक्ष्मः श्येनइव प्रापप्तद् वाचा साढः परस्तराम्।। 5:30:9

यो अग्ड.यो यः कर्ण्यो यो अक्ष्योर्विसल्पकः।
वि वृहामो विसल्पकं विद्रधं ह्रदयामयम्।
परा तमज्ञातं यक्ष्ममधराच्चं सुवामसि।। 6:127:3

आपो अग्रं दिव्या ओषधयः।
तास्तो यक्ष्ममेनस्य मग्ड.ादग्ड.दनीनशन्।। 8:7:3

तेनेममस्माद् यक्ष्मात् पुरूषं मुच्चतौषधीरथो कृणोमि भेषजम् 8:7:5

यस्य हेतोः प्रच्यवते यक्ष्मः कर्णत आस्यतः।
सर्वं शीर्षण्यं ते रोगं बहिर्निर्मन्त्रयामहे।। 9:8:3

हरिमाणं ते अग्डे.भ्योऽप्वामन्तरोदरात्।
यक्ष्मोधामन्तरात्मनो बहिर्निर्मन्त्रयामहे।। 9:8:9

आसो बलासो भवतु मूत्रं भवत्वामयत्।
यक्ष्माणां सर्वेषां विषं निरवोचमहं त्वत्।। 9:8:10

बहिर्बिलं निर्द्रवतु काहाबाहं तवोदरात्।
यक्ष्माणां सर्वेषां विषं निरवोचमहं त्वत्।। 9:8:11

ये अग्ड.ानि मदयन्ति यक्ष्मासो रोपणास्तव।
यक्ष्माणां सर्वेषां विषं निरवोचमहं त्वत्।। 9:8:19

Chapter 6

Yajna Therapy: A Boon to Mankind

Navneet[1], Prabhat[1], D.R. Khanna[2] and Dinesh Chandra[3]
[1]Department of Botany and Microbiology,
[2]Department of Zoology and Environmental Science,
[3]Department of Ved,
Gurukul Kangri University, Hardwar

The word 'Veda' itself signifies science or complete knowledge. The various branches of science mentioned in the Vedas are Astronomy, Geography, Arithmetic, Physics, Botany, Bacteriology etc. shows that Vedas are not merely books of prayers, but it is a store house of all round knowledge needed by human beings on the earth. The basic secrets of all such sciences are briefly contained in the Vedas. It is our duty to probe into these secrets and after understanding their significance through careful research and experiments, use them for the welfare of mankind. One such science is Yajna therapy which remain hidden in the past and Swami Dayanand Saraswati resurged the studies of Vedas and pointedly brought out that it is the duty of every human being to perform Yajna.

Yajna is found useful in the treatment of various diseases like tuberculosis, malaria, syphilis, skin diseases, asthma and fever etc. The microbial diseases must be due to anyone of the following causes:

1. The human blood has become impure.
2. The entry of microbes inside the body.
3. The malfunctioning of the internal organs of the body due to infection.

In order to get rid of these diseases various means are being used *e.g.* use of blood purifying medicines injections, vaccinations, consulting the doctor etc. Inspite of all these efforts the people are not satisfied. Our Rishis and munies of the Vedic era had found a complete cure of all such diseases. The yajna samagri is one of the devices used by them to cure the disease. In the yajna samagri giloyae, chirayata, honey etc. are used. These agents can be called as blood purifying agents as their atoms enter into the blood directly through respiration. Similarly, Guggul, tulsi, laung and other medicines are antimicrobial in their mode of action and destroy the microbes in the body. Ghee, akhroot, dakh, badam etc. makes the body healthy. Thus by using known and time tested medicinal plants in the samagri of the yajna we can enable ourselves to keep away from diseases caused by microbes. This reduces the chances of infection in the human body. It is remarkable to note that people infected with deadly diseases like tuberculosis, asthma, fever etc. can be cured by performing the yajna. It should be noted here that the medicines available in the market are also permitted to be used for the respective ailments.

Chronic diseases are difficult to be cured because the microbes after entering into the body get deposited inside the organs and slowly affect the body. In such cases it becomes difficult to kill the microbes and their large population with medicines as they have little effect on them. As a matter of fact the microform of a substance is more effective than its large, solid macroform. When we put the mixture of medicinal plants into fire, they are converted into infinite small particles unseen by the eyes and thus the properties of a plant are multiplied. After burning the medicinal herbs in fire they not only kill the microbes in the air of a room but also can show its effect far away. When they enter inside the body they can reach upto that part of the body where microbes are residing. They kill the microbes after entering the body through respiration. The smoke emitted out of yajna is not influenced by any external agent like season, air, person etc. It is beneficial to human body and mankind. Hence, they help in healing the body as soon as it comes in contact with this kind of atmosphere. Our Rishis have given a kind or blessing to those who perform yajna and live for hundred years as depicted in the following mantra:

शतं जीव शरदो वर्धमानः शतं।

हेमन्ताछवमु वसतान्।

शतं तइन्द्रो अग्निः सविता बृहस्पतिः

शतायुष हरिपाहार्ष मे नम्।। (ऋगवेद)

Table 6.1: Yajna Samagri to Cure Malaria

Sl.No.	*Common Name*	*Botanical Name*	*Family*	*Part Used*
1.	Guggal	*Commiphora mukul*	Burseraceae	Gum
2.	Giloya	*Tinospora cordifolia*	Menispermaceae	Whole plant
3.	Tulsi	*Ocimum sanctum*	Labiatae	Seeds
4.	Jaiphal	*Myristica fragrans*	Myristicaceae	Seeds
5.	Chirayita	*Swertia chirayita*	Gentianaceae	Whole plant
6.	Atis	*Aconitum heterophyllum*	Ranunculaceae	Root
7.	Shalparni	*Desmodium gangeticum*	Fabaceae	Whole plant
8.	Brahmi	*Centella asiatica*	Umbelliferae	Whole plant
9.	Makoi	*Zizyphus oenoplia*	Rhamnaceae	Whole plant
10.	Rose	*Rosa indica*	Rosaceae	Flower
11.	Laung	*Eugenia caryophyllata*	Myrtaceae	Fruits
12.	Mulahathi	*Glycyrrhiza glabra*	Leguminosae	Root
13.	Howber	*Juniperus communis*	Cupressaceae	Fruit
14.	Kapur	*Cinnamomum camphora*	Lauraceae	Wood (Gum)

Contd...

Table 6.1–Contd...

Sl.No.	*Common Name*	*Botanical Name*	*Family*	*Part Used*
15.	Akarkara	*Anacyclus pyrethrum*	Compositae	Root
16.	Sugar	*Saccharum album*	Graminaceae	Stem
17.	Masparni (Ood)	*Teramnus labialis*	Leguminosae	Whole plant
18.	Asgandh	*Withania somnifera*	Solanaceae	Root
19.	Sahora (Sihira)	*Streblus asper*	Moraceae	Bark
20.	Cow Ghee			

Table 6.2: Yajna Samagri to Cure Diabetes

Sl.No.	Common Name	Botanical Name	Family	Part Used
1.	Guggal	*Commiphora mukul*	Burseraceae	Gum
2.	Harad	*Terminalia chebula*	Combretaceae	Fruit
3.	Bahera	*Terminalia bellirica*	Combretaceae	Fruit
4.	Amla	*Emblica officinalis*	Euphorbiaceae	Fruit
5.	Til	*Sesamum indicum*	Pedaliaceae	Seed
6.	Giloya	*Tinospora cordifolia*	Menispermaceae	Whole plant
7.	Chandan	*Santalum album*	Santalaceae	Wood
8.	Jamun	*Syzygium cumini*	Myrtaceae	Fruits
9.	Gurmar	*Gymnema aurantiacum*	Asclepiadaceae	Leaves
10.	Bail	*Aegle marmelos*	Rutaceae	Fruits
11.	Gular	*Ficus glomerata*	Moraceae	Bark
12.	Honey			
13.	Cow Ghee			

Table 6.3: Yajna Samagri for Skin Diseases

Sl.No.	*Common Name*	*Botanical Name*	*Family*	*Part Used*
1.	Guggal	*Commiphora mukul*	Burseraceae	Gum
2.	Howber	*Juniperus communis*	Cupressaceae	Fruit
3.	Brahmi	*Centella asiatica*	Umbelliferae	Whole plant
4.	Neem	*Azadirachta indica*	Meliaceae	Leaves
5.	Giloya	*Tinospora cordifolia*	Menispermaceae	Whole plant
6.	Chirayita	*Swertia chirayita*	Gentianaceae	Whole plant
7.	Kapur	*Cinnamomum camphora*	Lauraceae	Stem
8.	Sulphur			
9.	Honey			
10.	Cow Ghee			

Table 6.4: Yajna Samagri to Cure Syphilis

Sl.No.	*Common Name*	*Botanical Name*	*Family*	*Part Used*
1.	Guggal	*Commiphora mukul*	Burseraceae	Gum
2.	Mundi	*Sphaeranthus indicus*	Compositae	Whole plant
3.	Chirayita	*Swertia chirayita*	Gentianaceae	Whole plant
4.	Khas	*Vetiveria zizanioidis*	Graminae	Root
5.	Kamal	*Nelumbo nucifera*	Nymphaceae	Seeds
6.	Singhara	*Trapa natans*	Trapaceae	Fruits
7.	Red chandan	*Pterocarpus santalinus*	Leguminosae	Wood
8.	White chandan	*Santalum album*	Santalaceae	Wood
9.	Gokhru	*Tribulus terrestris*	Zygophyllaceae	Fruit
10.	Brahmi	*Centella asiatica*	Umbelliferae	Whole plant
11.	Giloya	*Tinospora cordifolia*	Menispermaceae	Whole Plant
12.	Munakka	*Vitis vinifera*	Vitaceae	Fruits
13.	Devdar	*Cedrus deodara*	Pinaceae	Wood
14.	Honey			
15.	Cow Ghee			
16.	Triphla			

Table 6.5: Yajna Samagri for Tuberculosis

Sl.No.	Common Name	Botanical Name	Family	Part Used
1.	Guggal	*Commiphora mukul*	Burseraceae	Gum
2.	White chandan	*Santalum album*	Santalaceae	Wood
3.	Chirounji	*Bachanania lanzan*	Anacardiaceae	Flower
4.	Agar	*Aquilaria agallocha*	Thymelaeaceae	Wood
5.	Tagar	*Veleriana vellichi*	Valerianceae	Root
6.	Jaiphal	*Myristica fragrans*	Myristicaceae	Fruit
7.	Laung	*Eugenia caryophyllata*	Myrtaceae	Fruit
8.	Munakka	*Vitis vinifera*	Vitaceae	Fruit
9.	Kesmish	*Vitis vinifera*	Vitaceae	Fruit
10.	Haychi (bari)	*Amomum aromaticum*	Cannaceae	Fruit
11.	Rose	*Rosa indica*	Rosaceae	Flower
12.	Harad	*Terminalia chebula*	Combretaceae	Fruit
13.	Rice	*Oryza sativa*	Gramineae	Fruit
14.	Kapur	*Cinnamomum camphora*	Lauraceae	Stom (Gum)
15.	Sugar	*Saccharum album*	Gramineae	Stem
16.	Brahmi	*Centella asiatica*	Umbelliferae	Whole plant
17.	Shalparni	*Desmodium gangeticum*	Fabaceae	Whole plant
18.	Makoi	*Zizyphus oenoplia*	Rhamnaceae	Whole plant

Contd.

Table 6.5–Contd...

Sl.No.	Common Name	Botanical Name	Family	Part Used
18a.	Rasana	*Pluchea lanceolata*	Compositae	Leaves
19.	Jatamansi	*Nordostachys jatamansi*	Valerianaceae	Root
20.	Amla	*Emblica officinalis*	Euphorbiaceae	Fruit
21.	Pandri	*Randia uliginosa*	Rabiaceae	Whole plant
22.	Gokhru	*Tribulus terrestris*	Zygophyllaceae	Fruit
23.	Jivanti	*Leptadenia reticulata*	Asclepiadaceae	Stem
24.	Punarnava	*Boerhavia diffusa*	Nyctaginaceae	Stem
25.	Cheer	*Pinus roxburghii*	Pinaceae	Stem
26.	Khoob kalan	*Sisymbrium irio*	Cruciferae	Seed
27.	Jaun	*Ilordeum vulgae*	Gramineae	Fruit
28.	Til	*Sesamum indicum*	Pedaliaceae	Seed
29.	Shatawar	*Asparagus racemosus*	Liliaceae	Root
30.	Adusa (bisauta)	*Adhatoda vasica*	Acanthaceae	Whole plant
31.	Almond	*Prunus amygdahus*	Rosaceae	Seed
32.	Keshar	*Crocus sativus*	Iridaceae	Flower
33.	Honey			
34.	Seasonal fruits			
35.	Halwa			
36.	Cow Ghee			

Table 6.6: Yajna Samagri for Asthma

Sl.No.	Common Name	Botanical Name	Family	Part Used
1.	Guggal	*Commiphora mukul*	Burseraceae	Gum
2.	Giloya	*Tinospora cordifolia*	Menispermaceae	Whole Plant
3.	Triphala:			
	(a) Amla	*Emblica officinalis*	Euphorbiaceae	Fruit
	(h) Harad	*Terminalia chebula*	Combretaceae	Fruit
	(c) Bahera	*Terminalia bellirica*	Combretaceae	Fruit
4.	Agar	*Aquilaria agallocha*	Thymelaeaceae	Stem
5.	Tagar	*Valeriana wallichi*	Valerianaceae	Root
6.	Jatamansi	*Nordostachys jatamansi*	Valerianaceae	Root
7.	Mulathi	*Glycyrrhiza glabra*	Leguminosae	Root
8.	Munakka	*Vitis vinifera*	Vitaceae	Fruit
9.	Kapur	*Cinnamomum camphora*	Lauraceae	Gum
10.	Sugar	*Saccharum album*	Gramineae	Stem
11.	Cow Ghee			

The Yajna samagri to cure malaria, diabetes, syphilis, skin diseases, asthma and tuberculosis is given in Tables 6.1–6.6[1].

[1] Agnihotri, F.L., 1995. *Dev Yajya*. Vedic Pustakalaya, Dayanand Ashram, Ajmer.

Chapter 7

Vedic Science and Environment

Sudha Dubey
Department of Zoology,
Holkar Science College Indore, M.P.

In the Veda's natural elements play a pivot role but the international–ship of creation was always within the context of its relationship with the creator.

The Vedic sages believed that everything in this world stems from divine knowledge (the world) which was first revealed to the group of seers, who then passed this knowledge to successive generations of Vedic seers.

The Gala-hypothesis postulates that planet earth is a living organism that adjusts and regulates itself like any other organism, and that for 3.5 billion years, microbes, plant and animals have co-evolved with the environment as one globally integrated super organism. In much the same vein, Deep ecology believes in the essential ecological equality of all species man and mouse, elephant and earthworm. In an interconnected indivisible ecosystem each part is as crucial as the next.

The Vedas have categorically explains the role of nature, principle of food, life, intellect, and immortality. Earth, constellations and their roles are also defined in the Vedas. For sun and moon are celestial. God air, water and sky are aerial Gods. Earth, river and fire are the terrestrial God. The universe is composed of five elements earth, sky, water, wind and fire.

Vedic science urges people to pursue the path of ethical and sustainable economy, which coincides with the philosophy of ecological economics for sustainable development. The conventional economics always favours maximizing the material wealth so that individual will have a better quality of life.

This philosophy is incomplete from the environmental, spiritual and social point of view. Vedic philosophy equates the quality of life with both materialistic and non-materialistic values. The emerging theoretical notion of simple living in western culture is negative reaction to material wealth and positive inclination to ecological economics and strong sustainability. The gist of Vedas, are linear to with human and nature. Hence the present consumption based economy which believes the more you consume the more you will he better off, ignores the less consuming folks.

In the Vedic tradition, it is clearly stated that the life of each species is meant for well being of all other species, all of the 8,400,000 species on the planet live for each other except for one.

One species lives for itself and that is the human species. If the human species could also live accordingly to the laws of nature and in harmony with other species. The planet would become a very different place to live.

The sustainability rules of ecological economics are:

1. The rate of exploitation of renewable resources should not exceed the regeneration rate.
2. The pollution should be kept at or below the waste absorptive capacity of the environment. For degradable waste the rate of discharge should be less than the rate which ecosystem can absorb, whereas the persistent rate of discharges should be zero since the ecosystem has no capacity to assimilate such wastes.
3. The Extraction of non-renewable resources should be consistent with the development of renewable substitute.

Veda and Ecology

Earth is represented as goddess, which feeds everyone. All the forms of earth and of life on it are the children of earth. Rivers, trees animals are attendants of the earth goddess. The sun, moon, rain, wind and lightening are the children of sky. The sun is one of the three main deities of Vedas, which is at the center of creation and known as the nourisher.

The Rigveda says that sun is the soul of world. Between the earth and the sky, the abode of sun, is the sphere of sky and air – the cosmic life of breath. Fire is the other important deity of Vedas which serves the human from birth to death. Water is not only an element of purification but also the element pervading all life and thus a symbol of pervasiveness.

Veda and Biodiversity

The Vedas and Upanishads mention that the Gods and goddesses favour different biological resources. Knowledge of biodiversity, interrelation between living species and the environment, the need to maintain natural dynamism, and the natural way of transgressing the ecological principles are mentioned in *Yajur-veda*.

Similarly the Rigveda mentions about the forest goddess and healing properties of plants, tribes of fishes, goats, and etc. Cow is believed as thriomorphic animal in *Atharva-veda*. Hence, followers of Veda should avoid eating it.

In general practice, there are many flora and fauna which are sacred among the followers of the Vedas because they are directly or indirectly related with different Gods.

There are many sacred plants that Hindus worship regularly. For instance Tulsi, Rudrakchya, Bar, Pipal and Sāmi are the most religious plant species. In Rigveda Soma is mentioned as king of plants, there are hundreds of medicinal plants which are in use from Vedic period to now. This is one of the main economic activities *i.e.* harvesting of wild medicinal plants, of people living in the upper mountain areas of Nepal.

There are some ecological codes of conduct practiced among the followers of Vedas, one should always pray to the food, no one should disturb the habitat of wild animals, also trees should not be disturbed during night because of presence of God's soul in the tree trunk. Such rules are mentioned in the law of *Manu* (*Manusmriti*) and further catalogued by the Tiwari and Dwivedi.

According to the activist *Vandana Shiva's* book, *The Seed Keeper*, new seeds were first worshipped before being consumed. New crop was worshipped before being consumed. For the farmer, field is the mother: worshipping the field is a sign of gratitude towards the earth, who as mother feeds the millions of life forms who are her children.

In the place of chemical manures and pesticides, the traditional farmer used nature's own check and balances to nature fertility and keeps pests at bay.

A typical rice field supported and in some places continue to do so 800 species of "friendly insects"- spiders, wasps, ants and pathogens that controlled 95 per cent of insect pests.

These practices are still a living presence among India's tribal societies, for instance, the Warlis, a community near Mumbai worship nature of Hirva (green) and consider all produce to be gifts of Hirva, rather the fruits of their own labour.

Conservation of plants and animals was an innate aspect of their culture, illustrated in the concept of the secret grooves: mangroves, marshlands and other tracts of land supposedly inhabited by spirits, where killing of plants and animals is taboo.

The Bishnois of Rajasthan, too, will rather die than let a single tree be felled. The concept of coexistence took many forms. Before felling a tree to construct a temple carpenter traditionally saught the permission of the tree. And in Emperor Ashoka's time, veterinary hospitals were state institutions.

Conclusion

The Vedas are the primary sources of not only moral enhancement for the economic man but also paths for misguided ecology to achieve a true sustainability. It views human perfection and happiness from integrated perspectives, which embraces both material and spiritual values in individual and harmonious unity. The Vedas will guide to enlighten the inner human soul in order to maintain have moral values, true purpose of life and care for nature. The Vedic cultures are unique from development perspectives.

The Vedas have the potential of many remedies to the today's world problems of unsustainable development. For instance, "Dharma" is typical word in Hindu literature including Vedas and still in the Vedic cultures. It implies the sustainability, that is, if anyone violates the dharma, God may punish the violator, so no one will or should act against it. People save or even earn the dharma by visiting the temple or holy places in order to pave the way for heaven and have liberation, despite the multitude of sinful acts in other places. It seems that the modern act of Hindu people is also deviating from the Vedic philosophy, which is primarily due to the influence of "economic man".

It may sustain for a while, but not for the long term or strong sustainability. Hence, people need to have the real dharma, which loves nature and does not wish to rule over the nature, should be today's ideal philosophy for development.

Thus the Indian culture is suffused with deep affinity and unbounded reverence for nature. It is high time to wake up and be aware of this lofty and insightful life vision of our rishis. The modern development model of the society and the world is dramatically opposed to the view propounded by the rishis. To call it a product of demonic culture will not be entirely wrong.

Its ideal is reckless abuse of nature and maximum exploitation of its resources. The present crisis of environment degradation is the direct result of this merciless exploitation and ravishment of nature. As long as a sense of love and respect for nature is not developed, all materialistic efforts of environment protection would remain superficial and futile.

This is not possible without glimpsing the immanent presence of supreme being in each atom of creation. There can be no solution to the environmental crisis without bringing about a fundamental change in our outlook.

Facts and Figures of Change in Environment

During the last fifty years the percentage of dusty storm is increased five times in Asia, due to which natural calamity along with the health and economy problem has risen.

According to the survey of *"Forest Resource Assessment–2000"* nine million hectare part of world's forest is decreasing every year.

In the "September-2000" edition of a *"World Resource"* journal two-third of the world's total sea is polluted. The water level of earth also has been reduced.

One should not be surprised if today's stock exchange will be affected due to summer, rain clouds, etc. in future. Economist says that change in the nature like raindrops of rainy season, heat of summer and other beautiful parts of nature will affect the stock exchange from Mumbai to New York.

Although the rise in the economy of country from 1950–2000 has had been raised up to seven times but in return 50 per cent of fertile land has been changed into barren land.

Necessary steps should be taken in order to save our planet from the environmental pollution.

References

Akhand Jyothi (July–August), 2004. *Only the Rishi Vision.*

Everyman's Science, (June–July), 2004. *The Indian Science Journal,* Kolkata, 39(2).

Kapoor, Pramila. *Endangered Resources: Biodiversity and Cultural Knowledge.* Vijay and Stephen, Blackmore.

Niranjananand, Swami Ji. *Yoga and Ecology.*

Pachauri, S.K. *Workshop on Green Productivity and Bench Marking.*

Sahastrabuddhe, M.T. *Vedic Science Compared with Modern Science.*

Vajpayee, Kailash. *East to Eden.*

Chapter 8

Yajna Samagri for Different Seasons

Navneet[1], Prabhat[1] and Dinesh Chandra[2]
[1]Department of Botany and Microbiology,
[2]Department of Ved,
Gurukul Kangri University, Hardwar

Vedic yajna is based on the biorhythms of nature. Yajna produces specific effects in the atmosphere and has a certain therapeutic effects on human mind. The important part of vedic yajna is the samagri used in performing the yajna. The ingredients used in the yajna samagri have medicinal properties at the core of them. These properties get spread in the atmosphere after the performance of yajna and exactly synchronize the circadian rhythm corresponding to sunrise and sunset. This results in beneficial effects on the body, mind and wisdom of the persons performing the yajna. An atmosphere of tranquility, genial understanding and discipline develops. The atmosphere is filled with healthy nutrients and its fragrance pleases the mind. Moreover, the ingredients present inside the samagri plays an important role in controlling microbial population in the atmosphere. Thus the effect of yajna samagri on survival or saprophytic and pathogenic microbes in the atmosphere helps in treating air borne infections.

The yajna samagri for different seasons is given in Tables 8.1–8.6.

Method of Preparation of Yajna Samagri

The following points are taken into consideration at the time of preparation of yajna samagri:

1. The ingredients should be collected separately and kept in different labelled polythene bags. The ingredients must be authentic and pure. The old and rotten ingredients should not be used.
2. The fresh and green medicinal plants (*e.g. Tinospora cordifolia* etc.) are to be used in yajna samagri after cutting them into pieces and drying in the sunlight for one or two days.
3. The ingredients should be cut into small pieces and are to be mixed properly.
4. *Cinnamomum camphora* (Kapur), *Crocus sativus* (Kesar), *Myristica fragrans* (Javatri), sugar and ghee will be kept separately and are to be used as follows:
   (*a*) *Cinnamomum camphora* is to be used for the lightening of fire.
   (*b*) *Crocus sativus* and *Myristica fragrans* are to be mixed in ghee.

Table 8.1: Yajna Samagri for Sishir (Winter) Season, January–February

Sl.No.	*Common Name*	*Botanical Name*	*Family*	*Fart Used*	*Quantity per 100 gm*
1.	Akhroot	*Juglans regia*	Juglandaceae	Fruit	5 gm
2.	Kachur	*Curcuma zedoaria*	Zingiberaceae	Root	5 gm
3.	Viabidang	*Embelia ribes*	Myrsinaceae	Fruit	2 gm
4.	Guchmundi	*Gerwia hirsuta*	Tiliaceae	Bark	5 gm
5.	Mochras	*Salmalia malabarica*	Bombacaceae	Whole plant	2 gm
6.	Giloya	*Tinospora cordifolia*	Menispermaceae	Whole plant	2 gm
7.	Munakka	*Vitis vinifera*	Vitaceae	Fruit	5 gm
8.	Renuka (Nirgundi)	*Vitex negundo*	Verbenaceae	Whole plant	1 gm
9.	Kala Til	*Sesamum indicum*	Pedaliaceae	Seeds	5 gm
10.	Tajpatra	*Cinnamomum zeylanicum*	Lauraceae	Leaves	2 gm
11.	Keshar	*Crocus sativus*	Iridaceae	Flower	–
12.	Chandan	*Santalum album*	Santalaceae	Wood	5 gm
13.	Chirayita	*Swertia chirayita*	Gentianaceae	Stem	5 gm
14.	Kharjur	*Phoenix sylvestris*	Palmae	Fruit	5 gm
15.	Tulsi	*Ocimum sanctum*	Labiatae	Seed	2 gm

Contd...

Table 8.1–Contd...

Sl.No.	*Common Name*	*Botanical Name*	*Family*	*Part Used*	*Quantity per 100 gm*
16.	Guggal	*Commiphora mukul*	Burseraceae	Gum	10 gm
17.	Chirounji	*Bachanania lanzan*	Anacardiaceae	Seeds	2 gm
18.	Khand (Sugar)	*Saccharum album*	Gramineae	Stem	16 gm
19.	Kakdasingi	*Pistacia integerrima*	Anacardiaceae	Stem	2 gm
20.	Satawar	*Asparagus racemosus*	Liliaceae	Root	2 gm
21.	Daruhaldi	*Berberis aristata*	Berberidaceae	Root	2 gm
22.	Sankhpuspi	*Convolvulus pluricaulis*	Convolvulaceae	Whole plant	1 gm
23.	Padmakh	*Prunus cerasoides*	Rosaceae	Stem	2 gm
24.	Kaunch	*Mucuna prurita*	Leguminosae	Seeds	2 gm
25.	Jatamansi	*Nordostachys jatamansi*	Valerianaceae	Root	5 gm
26.	Bhojpatra	*Betula utilis*	Betulaceae	Stem	1 gm
27.	Kapur	*Cinnamomum camphora*	Lauraceae	Stem	2 gm
28.	Halwa				
29.	Ghee (Cow)				

Table 8.2: Yajna Samagri for Basant (Spring) Season, March–April

Sl.No.	Common Name	Botanical Name	Family	Part Used	Quantity per 100 gm
1.	Chhadila	*Permelia perlata*	Parmeliaceae	Whole plant	4 gm
2.	Talispatra	*Abies webbiana*	Pinaceae	Leaves	2 gm
3.	Dakh	*Vitis vinifera*	Vitaceae	Fruit	2 gm
4.	Lajjavanti	*Mimosa pudica*	Leguminosae	Whole plant	2 gm
5.	Seetalchini	*Piper cubeba*	Piperaceae	Fruit	4 gm
6.	Kapur	*Cinnamomum camphora*	Lauraceae	Stem	2 gm
7.	Cheer	*Pinus roxburghii*	Pinaceae	Wood	2 gm
8.	Devdar	*Cedrus deodara*	Pinaceae	Wood	2 gm
9.	Giloya	*Tinospora cordifolia*	Menispermaceae	Whole plant	4 gm
10.	Agar	*Aquilaria agallocha*	Thymelaeaceae	Stem	2 gm
11.	Tagar	*Valeriana vellichii*	Velerianceae	Root	2 gm
12.	Kesar	*Crocus sativus*	Iridaceae	Flowers	–
13.	Indrajau	*Holarrhena antidysenterica*	Apocynaceae	Seeds	2 gm
14.	Guggal	*Commiphora mukul*	Burseraceae	Gum	10 gm
15.	Chandan	*Santalum album*	Santalaceae	Wood	2 gm

Contd...

Table 8.2–Contd...

Sl.No.	Common Name	Botanical Name	Family	Part Used	Quantity per 100 gm
16.	Javitri	*Myristica fragrans*	Myristiaceae	Flower	2 gm
17.	Jaiphal	*Myristica fragrans*	Myristiaceae	Fruit	2 gm
18.	Dhoob	*Cynodon dactylon*	Gramineae	Whole plant	4 gm
19.	Sarson	*Brassica campestris*	Cruciferae	Seeds	4 gm
20.	Puskarmule	*Inula racemosa*	Compositae	Root	4 gm
21.	Kamal	*Nelumbo nucifera*	Nymphaeaceae	Seeds	2 gm
22.	Mangistha	*Rubia cordifolia*	Rubiaceae	Root	2 gm
23.	Dalchini	*Cinnamomum zeylanicum*	Lauraceae	Stem	4 gm
24.	Gular (bark)	*Ficus glomerata*	Moraceae	Stem	2 gm
25.	Tajbal	*Zanthoxylum armatum*	Rutaceae	Fruit	4 gm
26.	Sankhpushpi	*Convolvulus pluricaulis*	Convolvulaceae	Whole plant	2 gm
27.	Chirayita	*Swertia chirayita*	Gentianaceae	Stem	4 gm
28.	Khas	*Vetiveria zizanioidis*	Gramineae	Root	4 gm
29.	Gokhru	*Tribulus terrestris*	Zygophyllaceae	Fruit	4 gm
30.	Khand	*Saccharum ablum*	Gramineae	Stem	12 gm
31.	Seasonal fruit				
32.	Ghee (Cow)				

Table 8.3: Yajna Samagri for Grisma (Summer) Season, May–June

Sl.No.	*Common Name*	*Botanical Name*	*Family*	*Part Used*	*Quantity per 100 gm*
1.	Mura (murva)	*Marsdenia tenacissima*	Asclepiadaceae	Root	4 gm
2.	Viabidang	*Embelia ribes*	Myrsinaceae	Fruit	4 gm
3.	Kapur	*Cinnamomum camphora*	Lauraceae	Stem	4 gm
4.	Nagar motha	*Cyperus rotundus*	Cyperaceae	Root	4 gm
5.	Pila (pilu)	*Salvadora persica*	Salvadoraceae	Whole plant	2 gm
6.	Chandan	*Santalum album*	Santalaceae	Wood plant	4 gm
7.	Chhadila	*Parmelia perlata*	Parmeliaceae	Whole plant	4 gm
8.	Nirmali	*Strychnos potatorum*	Loganiaceae	Seed	4 gm
9.	Shatawar	*Asparagus racemosus*	Liliaceae	Root	4 gm
10.	Khas	*Vitiveria zizanioides*	Gramineae	Root	2 gm
11.	Giloya	*Tinospora cordifolia*	Manispermaceae	Whole plant	4 gm
12.	Dhoob (Dub)	*Cynodon dactylon*	Gramineae	Whole plant	4 gm
13.	Dalchini	*Cinnamomum zeylanicum*	Lauraceae	Leaves, stem	4 gm
14.	Laung	*Eugenia caryophylata*	Myrtaceae	Fruit	2 gm
15.	Tagar	*Valerianaceae wallichii*	Valerianaceae	Root	4 gm

Contd...

Table 8.3–Contd...

Sl.No.	*Common Name*	*Botanical Name*	*Family*	*Part Used*	*Quantity per 100 gm*
16.	Bhojpatra	*Betula utilis*	Betulaceae	Leaves	2 gm
17.	Rice	*Oryza sativa*	Gramineae	Fruit	16 gm
18.	Kush (root)	*Desmostachya bipinnata*	Gramineae	Root	4 gm
19.	Talishpatra	*Abies webbiana*	Pinaceae	Leaves	2 gm
20.	Padmakh	*Prunus cerasoides*	Rosaceae	Stem	4 gm
21.	Daruhaldi	*Berberis aristata*	Berberidaceae	Root	4 gm
22.	Mangistha	*Rubia cordifolia*	Rubiaceae	Root	4 gm
23.	Shilaras	*Liquidamber orientalis*	Hamamelidaceae	Gum	4 gm
24.	Kesar	*Crocus sativus*	Iridaceae	Flower	–
25.	Jatamansi	*Nordostachys jatamansi*	Valerianaceae	Root	4 gm
26.	Ilaychi	*Elettaria cardamomum*	Zingiberaceae	Fruit	2 gm
27.	Ghee (Cow)				

Table 8.4: Yajna Samagri for Varsa (Rainy) Season, July–August

Sl.No.	Common Name	Botanical Name	Family	Part Used	Quantity per 100 gm
1.	Agar	*Aquilaria agallocha*	Thumelaceae	Stem	2 gm
2.	Jaun	*Hordeum vulgare*	Gramineae	Fruit	2 gm
3.	Cheer	*Pinus roxburghii*	Pinaceae	Wood	2 gm
4.	Doob	*Cynodon dactylon*	Gramineae	Whole plant	2 gm
5.	Sarson	*Brassica campestris*	Cruciferae	Seed	2 gm
6.	Tagar	*Valeriana wallichii*	Valerianaceae	Root	2 gm
7.	Devdaru	*Cedrus deodora*	Pinaceae	Wood	2 gm
8.	Guggal	*Commiphora mukul*	Burseraceae	Gum	20 gm
9.	Nakchikni	*Centipeda minima*	Compositae	Seed	4 gm
10.	Sal (Shal)	*Shorea robusta*	Depterocarpaceae	Gum	4 gm
11.	Jayaphal	*Myristica fragrans*	Myristicaceae	Fruit	4 gm
12.	Nirmali	*Strychnos potatorum*	Loganiaceae	Seed	4 gm
13.	Makhane	*Euryale ferox*	Nymphaeaceae	Fruit	4 gm
14.	Tajpatra	*Cinnamomum tamala*	Lauraceae	Leaves	2 gm
15.	Kapur	*Cinnamomum camphora*	Lauraceae	Stem	2 gm

Contd...

Table 8.4–Contd...

Sl.No.	*Common Name*	*Botanical Name*	*Family*	*Part Used*	*Quantity per 100 gm*
16.	Bail	*Aegle marmelos*	Rutaceae	Bark	4 gm
17.	Jatamansi	*Nordostachys jatamansi*	Valerianaceae	Root	2 gm
18.	Ilaychi (chhoti)	*Elettaria cardamomum*	Zingiberaceae	Fruit	4 gm
19.	Bach	*Acorus calamus*	Araceae	Root	2 gm
20.	Giloya	*Tinospora cordifolia*	Manispermaceae	Whole plant	4 gm
21.	Tulsi	*Ocimum sanctum*	Labiatae	Seeds	2 gm
22.	Viabidang	*Embelia ribes*	Myrinaceae	Fruit	2 gm
23.	Kamal	*Nelumbo nucifera*	Nymphaceae	Seeds	2 gm
24.	Chandan	*Santalum album*	Santalaceae	Wood	4 gm
25.	Nagkesar	*Mesua ferrea*	Guttiferae	Flower	2 gm
26.	Brahami	*Centella asiatica*	Umbelliferae	Whole plant	4 gm
27.	Chirayta	*Swertia chirayita*	Gentianaceae	Stem	2 gm
28.	Chuhare	*Phoenix sylvestris*	Plamae	Fruit	2 gm
29.	Sugar	*Saccharum album*	Gramineae	Stem	4 gm
30.	Rice	*Oryza sativa*	Gramineae	Fruit	2 gm
31.	Ghee (Cow)				

Table 8.5: Yajna Samagri for Sharad (Winter) Season, September–October

Sl.No.	*Common Name*	*Botanical Name*	*Family*	*Part Used*	*Quantity per 100 gm*
1.	White chandan	*Santalum album*	Santalaceae	Wood	4 gm
2.	Guggal	*Commiphora mukul*	Burseraceae	Gum	12 gm
3.	Nagkesar	*Mesua ferrea*	Guttiferae	Flower	4 gm
4.	Ilaychi (bari)	*Amomum aromaticum*	Cannaceae	Fruit	2 gm
5.	Giloya	*Tinospora cordifolia*	Menispermaceae	Whole plant	2 gm
6.	Chirounji	*Buchanania lanzan*	Anacardiaceae	Seed	4 gm
7.	Vidarikand	*Pueraria tuberosa*	Leguminosae	Root	4 gm
8.	Gular	*Ficus glomerata*	Moraceae	Bark	4 gm
9.	Brahami	*Centella asiatica*	Umbelliferae	Whole plant	6 gm
10.	Dalchini	*Cinnamomum zeylanicum*	Lauraceae	Stem	2 gm
11.	Kapur	*Cinnamomum camphora*	Lauraceae	Stem	4 gm
12.	Mochras	*Salmalia malabarica*	Bombacaceae	Whole plant	2 gm
13.	Pittpapra	*Fumaria vaillantii*	Fumariaceae	Whole plant	2 gm
14.	Agar	*Aquilaria agallocha*	Thymeloacaceae	Stem	2 gm
15.	Indrajaw	*Holarrhena antidysenterica*	Apocynaceae	Seed	2 gm

Contd...

Table 8.5–Contd...

Sl.No.	*Common Name*	*Botanical Name*	*Family*	*Part Used*	*Quantity per 100 gm*
16.	Ranuka (Nirgundi)	*Vitex negundo*	Verbenaceae	Whole plant	2 gm
17.	Munakka	*Vitis vinifera*	Vitaceae	Fruit	4 gm
18.	Asvagandha	*Withania somnifera*	Solanaceae	Root	2 gm
19.	Sheetal chini	*Piper cubeba*	Piperaceae	Fruit	2 gm
20.	Jaiphal	*Myristica fragrans*	Myristicaceae	Fruit	4 gm
21.	Chirayata	*Swertia chirayita*	Gentianaceae	Stem	2 gm
22.	Keshar	*Crocus sativus*	Iridaceae	Flower	–
23.	Kesmish	*Vitis vinifera*	Vitaceae	Fruit	4 gm
24.	Khand	*Saccharum album*	Gramineae	Stem	2 gm
25.	Jatamansi	*Nordostchys jatamansi*	Valerianaceae	Root	4 gm
26.	Tal Makhana	*Asteracantha longifolia*	Acanthaceae	Whole plant	2 gm
27.	Sehdevi	*Vernonia cineria*	Compositae	Whole plant	2 gm
28.	Dhak	*Butea monosperma*	Leguminosae	Bark	2 gm
29.	Kapur Kachri	*Hedychium spicatium*	Zingiberaceae	Root	4 gm
30.	Kheer	–	–		4 gm
31.	Vishnukanta	–	–		2 gm
32.	Ghee (Cow)				

Table 8.6: Yajna Samagri for Hemant (Cold Winter) Season, November–December

Sl.No.	Common Name	Botanical Name	Family	Part Used	Quantity per 100 gm
1.	Kuth	*Saussurea lappa*	Compositae	Root	2 gm
2.	Safed musli	*Asparagus adscendens*	Liliaceae	Root	2 gm
3.	Kokila	*Asteracantha longifolia*	Acanthaceae	Whole plant	4 gm
4.	Kapur kachri	*Hedychium spicatium*	Zingiberaceae	Root	4 gm
5.	Nakchikni	*Centipeda minima*	Compositae	Seed	2 gm
6.	Giloya	*Tinospora cordifolia*	Manispermaceae	Whole plant	2 gm
7.	Dalchini	*Cinnamomum zeylanicum*	Lauraceae	Stem	2 gm
8.	Bharngi (Jhangi)	*Lerodendrum serratum*	Verbenaceae	Root	4 gm
9.	Sounph	*Foeniculum vulgare*	Umbelliferae	Fruit	4 gm
10.	Munnaka	*Vitis vinifera*	Vitaceae	Fruit	2 gm
11.	Cheer	*Pinus roxburghii*	Pinaceae	Wood	4 gm
12.	Guggal	*Commiphora mukul*	Burseraceae	Gum	18 gm
13.	Akhroot	*Juglans regia*	Juglandaceae	Fruit	4 gm
14.	Rasna	*Pluchca lanceolata*	Compositae	Leaves	2 gm
15.	Pushkarmul	*Inula racemosa*	Compositae	Root	4 gm

Contd...

Table 8.6–Contd...

Sl.No.	*Common Name*	*Botanical Name*	*Family*	*Part Used*	*Quantity per 100 gm*
16.	Keshar	*Crocus sativus*	Iridaceae	Flower	–
17.	Chuhara	*Phoenix sylvestris*	Palmae	Fruit	4 gm
18.	Gokhru	*Tribulus terrestris*	Zygophyllaceae	Fruit	4 gm
19.	Kounch (Seed)	*Mucuna prurita*	Leguminosae	Seed	4 gm
20.	Pittpapra	*Fumaria vaillantii*	Fumariaceae	Whole plant	2 gm
21.	Mulhati	*Glycyrrhiza glabra*	Leguminosae	Root	2 gm
22.	Kaletil	*Linum usitatissimum*	Linaceae	Seed	4 gm
23.	Javitri	*Myristica fragrans*	Myristicaceae	Flower	2 gm
24.	Chandan	*Santalum album*	Santalaceae	Wood	2 gm
25.	Tagar	*Valeriana wallichi*	Valerianaceae	Root	4 gm
26.	Talish patra	*Abies webbiana*	Pinaceae	Leaves	2 gm
27.	Ranuka (Nirgundi)	*Vitex negundo*	Verbenaceae	Seed	4 gm
28.	Honey	–	–		4 gm
29.	Badam	–	–		2 gm
30.	Ghee (Cow)				

(*c*) As per the requirements of the yajna samagri, sugar, kapur, honey etc. should be mixed.

(*d*) Pure ghee is to be added in sufficient quantity, so that the yajna samagri does not give a dry appearance.

5. Cow's ghee is the most important and essential ingredient prescribed in the performance of yajna as ordained by the Vedas. In case it is not available then buffalow's ghee can be used but refined vanaspati ghee for performing yajna is highly improper and harmful.

Chapter 9
The Antimicrobial Effects of Agnihotra

Navneet, Prabhat and Amit
Department of Botany and Microbiology,
Gurukul Kangri University, Hardwar – 249 404

ABSTRACT

The antimicrobial effects of Agnihotra on the aeromicroflora of Prarthana Bhawan of Gurukul Kangri University were studied by using culture plate method. The density of bacteria and fungi was higher outside as compared to inside the Bhawan. The density of microbes decreases drastically inside the room after the performance of Agnihotra while it increases outside the room. The effect of Agnihotra on microbial population was observed even after five hours. Qualitatively a total of 14 fungal forms belonging to 9 genera were trapped from the air. *Cladosporium* was the chief constituent followed by *Aspergillus, Penicillium, Alternaria, Curvularia, Fusarium, Mucor, Rhizopus* and *Trichoderma.*

Keywords: *Aeromicroflora, Antimicrobial, Agnihotra.*

Introduction

A wide variety of microorganisms are present in the atmosphere. The air always contains spores but their number and types depend on the time of day, weather, season and geographical location (Gregory, 1961). Agnihotra is the smallest form of Vedic Homa. This sacrificial fire is a traditional antipollution ritual performed daily by a house holder. The Agnihotra produces certain specific effects in the atmosphere (Navneet *et al.,* 1988). The burning of medicinal herbs in fire kill the microbes in the air and thus help in healing the body as soon as it comes in contact with this kind of atmosphere (Navneet *et al.,* 2003). In the present study the effect of Agnihotra on the aeromicroflora of Prarthana Bhawan of Gurukul Kangri University has been investigated.

Materials and Methods

The antimicrobial effects of Agnihotra on the aeromicroflora of Prarthana Bhawan were studied by using culture plate method. Four petri dishes at three feet height containing Martin's agar medium were exposed for five minutes at four corners of the room, one petri dish in the centre and one outside the room to record the aeromycroflora. Similary, six petri dishes containing Nutrient agar medium were used to record the bacterial population. The first sampling was conducted one hour before the starting of yajna, the second sampling was done after five minutes of the flame time and the third sampling after five hours of closing time. The plates were incubated for *two* days at 37°C for quantitative estimation of bacteria and at 28°C for both quantitative and qualitative estimation of fungi.

Results and Discussion

The microflora of air inside and outside the Prarthana Bhawan was rich both quantitatively and qualitatively. The density of bacteria and fungi is given in Tables 9.1 and 9.2. The density of bacteria outside the Prarthana Bhawan was found to be higher as compared to inside in all the samplings. The density of bacteria decreases drastically inside the room after the performance of Agnihotra while it increases outside the room. Moreover, it was observed that the bacterial population inside the room was low even after five hours as shown in last sampling at 3.30 p.m. Similar trend was observed in case of fungi.

Qualitatively a total of 14 fungal forms belonging to 9 genera were trapped from the air (Tables 9.3 and 9.4). *Cladosporium* formed the main bulk of the total aeromycoflora which was represented by its two species *viz., C. cladosporioides* and *C. herbarum. C. cladosporioides* was found in maximum numbers. *Aspergillus* was the next abundant genus and is represented by four species *viz., A. flavus, A. niger, A. terreus* and unidentified *Aspergillus* sp. it is followed by *Penicillium cyclopium*. The other abundant colonies were those of *Alternaria alternata, Curvularia lunata, Fusarium equiseti, Mucor* sp., *Rhizopus oryzae, Trichoderma* and white sterile form.

Table 9.1: The Density of Bacteria per 100cm^3 in Prarthana Bhawan of Gurukul Kangri Vishwavidyalaya, Hardwar

Sampling Time	Date and Place									
	4/08/2003		19/09/2003		6/11/2003		15/12/2003		28/02/2004	
	Inside	Outside	Inside	Outside	Inside	Outside	Inside	Outside	Inside	Outside
9.30 A.M.	13.19	20.42	37.71	94.28	38.96	107.13	129.79	188.56	38.65	54.99
10.30 A.M.	7.8	47.14	8.48	140.85	23.25	150.84	108.1	204.27	28.91	56.56
3.30 P.M.	5.65	39.15	6.91	157.13	16.65	157.13	29.85	172.84	13.84	59.71

Table 9.2: The Density of Fungi per 100cm^3 in Prarthana Bhawan of Gurukul Kangri Vishwavidyalaya, Hardwar

Sampling Time	Date and Place									
	4/08/2003		19/09/2003		6/11/2003		15/12/2003		28/02/2004	
	Inside	Outside	Inside	Outside	Inside	Outside	Inside	Outside	Inside	Outside
9.30 A.M.	31.74	18.85	28.28	29.85	79.5	56.56	63.48	78.56	50.91	100.56
10.30 A.M.	12.88	54.99	16.97	50.28	54.68	56.42	32.39	81.7	44.91	109.99
3.30 P.M.	7.8	55.92	13.19	47.14	52.16	116.27	4.79	47.14	38.23	84.85

Table 9.3(a): Percentage Abundance of Aeromycoflora Inside the Prarthana Bhawan of Gurukul Kangri University, Hardwar

Name of Organisms	*Sampling Numbers, Date and Sampling Time*								
	I			*II*			*III*		
	4/8/2003			*19/09/03*			*6/11/2003*		
	9.30 A.M.	*10.30 A.M.*	*3.30 P.M.*	*9.30 A.M.*	*10.30 A.M.*	*3.30 P.M.*	*9.30 A.M.*	*10.30 A.M.*	*3.30 P.M.*
Alternaria alternata	6.93	–	–	3.4	3.7	4.68	7.5	7.9	5.59
Aspergillus flavus	17.82	19.51	20	2.27	1.85	4.68	9.09	31.63	23.63
A. niger	–	–	–	2.27	11.11	3.12	7.9	10.16	4.96
A. terreus	–	–	–	2.27	5.55	4.68	8.69	6.21	3.72
Aspergillus sp.	–	–	–	–	–	–	6.91	4.51	6.21
Cladosporium cladosporioides	25.74	34.14	36	34.09	31.25	31.25	24.5	15.26	19.39
C. herbarum	–	–	–	7.95	7.81	7.81	13.43	6.21	3.72
Curvularia lunata	–	–	–	2.27	–	–	–	–	–
Fusarium equiseti	7.92	9.75	12	–	–	–	0.39	–	–
Mucor sp.	15.84	14.63	16	9.09	–	1.56	7.9	9.03	16.14
Penicillium cyclopium	16.83	17.07	16	27.27	33.33	37.5	7.9	5.08	14.28
Rhizopus oryzae	8.91	2.43	–	–	–	–	–	–	–
Trichoderma sp.	–	–	–	–	–	–	–	0.56	0.62
White sterile form	–	2.43	–	9.09	5.55	4.68	5.92	3.38	3.72

Table 9.3(b): Percentage Abundance of Aeromycoflora Inside the Prarthana Bhawan of Gurukul Kangri University, Hardwar

Name of Organisms	*Sampling Numbers, Date and Sampling Time*					
	IV			*V*		
	15/12/03			*28/02/04*		
	9.30 A.M.	*10.30 A.M.*	*3.30 P.M.*	*9.30 A.M.*	*10.30 A.M.*	*3.30 P.M.*
Alternaria alternata	2.98	4.83	–	4.65	1.26	–
Aspergillus flavus	17.91	4.83	6.25	14.53	21.51	22.03
A. niger	10.94	9.67	6.25	5.81	12.65	11.86
A. terreus	19.9	27.14	31.25	19.18	12.65	13.55
Aspergillus sp.	–	6.45	–	–	–	–
Cladosporium cladosporioides	18.9	17.74	25	7.55	5.06	5.08
C. herbarum	11.94	14.51	6.25	5.81	5.06	3.38
Curvularia lunata	–	–	–	–	–	–
Fusarium equiseti	–	–	–	–	–	–
Mucor sp.	7.46	8.06	6.25	9.88	11.39	11.86
Penicillium cyclopium	3.48	–	6.25	10.46	10.12	8.47
Rhizopus oryzae	1.49	–	6.25	–	–	–
Trichoderma sp.	–	–	–	–	–	–
White sterile form	4.97	6.45	6.25	22.09	20.25	23.72

Table 9.4(a): Percentage Abundance of Aeromycoflora Outside the Prarthana Bhawan of Gurukul Kangri University, Hardwar

Name of Organisms	Sampling Numbers, Date and Sampling Time								
	I			II			III		
	4/8/2003			19/09/03			6/11/2003		
	9.30 A.M.	*10.30 A.M.*	*3.30 P.M.*	*9.30 A.M.*	*10.30 A.M.*	*3.30 P.M.*	*9.30 A.M.*	*10.30 A.M.*	*3.30 P.M.*
Alternaria alternata	75	17.14	–	13.33	7.4	10	5.55	7.27	1.35
Aspergillus flavus	16.66	14.28	5.26	20	6.17	16.66	16.66	5.45	50
A. niger	–	–	5.26	–	8.64	20	2.77	3.63	4.05
A. terreus	–	–	–	–	4.93	6.66	2.77	10.9	8.1
Aspergillus sp.	–	–	–	–	–	–	8.33	9.9	9.45
Cladosporium cladosporioides	–	25.71	36.84	26.66	24.69	6.66	22.22	18.18	13.51
C. herbarurm	–	–	5.26	13.33	6.17	6.66	19.44	–	2.7
Curvularia lunata	–	–	–	–	–	–	–	–	–
Fusarium equiseti	–	14.28	–	–	–	–	–	–	–
Mucor sp.	8.33	8.57	10.52	–	3.7	3.33	13.88	10.9	5.4
Penicillium cyclopium	–	8.57	36.84	16.66	33.33	10	2.77	–	4.05
Rhizopus oryzae	–	8.57	–	–	–	–	–	–	–
White sterile form	–	2.85	–	10	4.93	20	5.55	12.92	1.35

Table 9.4(b): Percentage Abundance of Aeromycoflora Outside the Prarthana Bhawan of Gurukul Kangri University, Hardwar

Name of Organisms	Sampling Numbers, Date and Sampling Time					
	IV			V		
	15/12/03			28/02/04		
	9.30 A.M.	10.30 A.M.	3.30 P.M.	9.30 A.M.	10.30 A.M.	3.30 P.M.
Alternaria alternata	–	5.55	–	6.09	14.93	–
Aspergillus flavus	18	25.92	6.66	12.19	12.5	7.4
A. niger	8	5.55	23.33	14.63	10.93	12.96
A. terreus	40	18.51	10	12.19	14.06	24.07
Aspergillus sp.	–	–	–	–	–	–
Cladosporium cladosporioides	16	14.81	6.66	12.19	14.93	22.22
C. herbarurm	6	3.7	10	6.09	15.62	–
Curvularia lunata	–	–	–	6.09	–	9.25
Fusarium equiseti	–	–	–	–	–	–
Mucor sp.	8	3.7	16.66	3.65	9.37	9.25
Penicillium cyclopium	?	5.55	16.05	8.53	7.81	5.55
Rhizopus oryzae	2	9.5	3.33	–	–	–
White sterile form	–	9.25	6.66	18.29	17.18	9.25

The samagri (herbal mixture) for different seasons (Navneet *et al.*, 2004) was prepared and used to perform the Agnihotra. The antimicrobial properties of medicinal herbs *i.e.* guggal, chirayata, giloya, kapoor, jaiphal, tagar, chandan etc. (Ahmed *et al.*, 1999; Perez and Anesini, 1994) used in the samagri are well known. The chemical reaction occur during the combustion of cow ghee, cereals, sugars and herbal ingredients offered as oblations to the fire in havan kunda. It produces gases like ethylene oxide, propylene oxide, formaldehyde, butapropiolactone etc. have their own germicidal values (Parkhe, 1982). The reduction in microbial count is due to fumigation effect and also by controlling the metabolic activity of microorganisms. Moreover, the uttering of the mantras produce vibrations and spread subtle energies in the surrounding atmosphere as the oblation are being offered. The emerging of red, yellow, blue colours of the flame and heat resulting from the burning of oblations has a unifying link which results in decreasing the microbial population.

References

Ahmad, I., Zaiba, Beg, A.Z. and Mehmood, Z., 1999. Antimicrobial potency of selected medicinal plants with special interest in activity against phytopathogenic fungi. *Indian Vet. Med. Jour.*, 3: 299–306.

Gregory, P.H., 1961. *The Microbiology of Atmosphere*, 1st edn. Wiley Interscience, New York, pp. 251.

Navneet, Chand, S. and Sharma, V.K., 1998. Agnihotra: The air purifier. *Gurukula Kangri Vijnana Patika Arybhata*, 1: 83–86.

Navneet, Prabhat and Chandra, D., 2003. Yajna Therapy: Its relevance in modern context. *Vedic Path.*, 61: 49–55.

Navneet, Prabhat and Chandra, D., 2004. *Yajna Samagri for Different Seasons*. Accepted–Gurukula Shodh Bharti, Gurukul Kangri University, Haridwar.

Parkhe, M.S., 1982. *Agnihotra*. Vaidika Samsodhana Mandala, Poona.

Perez, C. and Anesini, C., 1994. *In vitro* antibacterial activity of Argentine folk medicinal plants against *Salmonella typhii*. *Journal of Ethnopharmacology*, 44: 41–46.

Chapter 10

Approach to Cure Tamak Shwas (Asthma) by Panchkarma

Arun Chugh*
Navoday Ayurved and Panchkarma,
A-29, Sri Ram Nagar Colony,
Opposite Railway Station, Jwalapur – 249 407,
Haridwar, U.A.

ABSTRACT

In modern medicine, Asthma has no specific medicine to cure, so claimed as incurable disease. Ayurved believes that 'Sum dosh-Sum agni-Sum dhatu' (Primary bio-factors which carry out metabolism of the body) develops strong immune system. Ayurveda

* Member of Asthma and Bronchitis Association of India; Panchkarma Expert; Phone: 9219838164.

treatment consist in restoring of harmony between the Tridosha theory of Kapph, Pitta and Vata *i.e* Growth factor of life, Consuming factor of life and Motive factor of life. A study over 120 cases of Tamak Shwas was conducted at Navoday Ayurved and Panchkarma Centre. The cure rate was observed by the herbal and panchkarma treatment at different age group.

Introduction

Tamak Shwas or Asthma due to allergy is a chronic disease, characterized by inflammation the airways. The inflammation causes associated increase in the existing airway hyper responsiveness to variety of stimuli, such as allergens, cold air and virus. Exposure of the patient to these stimuli provokes a variety of changes in airways including broncho constriction, wheezing, breathlessness, chest, tightness and coughing experience by the patients with Asthma, particularly at night and in early morning, is usually associated with airflow obstruction.

Maharishi Charak illustrates the symptoms of shwas rog as:

प्रतिलोम यदा वायुः स्त्रोतासि प्रतिपद्यते ।
ग्रीवा शिरस्व संग हय श्लष्माणं समुदीय च ।।

(चरक—चि0 स्थान 54—91)

Asthma can occur at any age and individuals with its difference in frequency and degree of symptoms. Some people have only an occasional attack *i.e.* mild in degree and of brief duration and otherwise are entirely free of symptoms. Other have mild coughing and wheezing most of the time, triggered by several attacks following exposure to known allergen, infection or certain stress conditions.

Asthma can go unnoticed in people with the history of any allergic disorder who suffer from recurrent wheezing.

Ayurveda the ancient system of medicine believes in prevention from the disease. It has versatile approach to root out many incurable problems.

In Ayurveda, Asthma is known as Shwas Rog. It is described as:

1. Maha Shwas
2. Urdhva Shwas
3. Chhina Shwas
4. Tamak Shwas
5. Ksudra Shwas

Among these five types of Shwas first three are fatal and not curable. The last two Tamak and Ksudra Shwas are curable. More than 70 per cent of Asthma cases belong to Tamak Shwas and Ksudra Shwas group.

Samprapty of Tamak Shwas

दोष – कफ, पित्त

दूष्य – रस

स्त्रोतस – रसवह, प्राणवह

अग्नि – जठराग्नि एवं रसाग्नि

आम – जठराग्निजन्य एवं रसाग्निजन्य

व्याधि – क्षमत्व, अल्प

Patients and Methods

At Navoday Ayurved and Panchkarma Centre, situated near bank of Ganges, Jwalapur, Haridwar (U.A.). 120 cases of Tamak Shwas, from different part of India and of different age group was included in the study.

1. Age: 10 yrs to 75 year
2. Sex M/F: 72/48
3. Weight: 15 Kg to 92 Kg
4. Duration of illness: 6 months–20 yrs
5. Alcoholic addiction: 12 per cent
6. Tobacoo addiction: 10 per cent

Treatment was started by appointment for panchkarma.

During Acuteness

1. Oleation–Applied luke warm sesame eoil with a pint of rock salt over the chest and back region.
2. 1 grain of Asafoetida in water applied on navel region softly.
3. Kept both feets in salted hot water
4. Zinger Powder–1/4th teaspoon

   Black pepper–6 in nos. (Powder)

   Black salt–1/4th teaspoon

   Holy basil–5 in 4 number

   Somlata powder–½ teaspoon

The mixture was boiled in 200 ml of water and reduce to 50 ml. Filtered and given to sip.

For Childrens

Zinger juice–1 teaspoon

Basil leaves juice–1 teaspoon

Honey–1 teaspoon

Warm water–½ cup

This mixture was given 2–3 times a day.

During Normal Phase

Internal Oleation–Vasa Ghrit in Khiedi was given in following order.

1st day–25 ml.

2nd day–50 ml.

3rd day–75 ml.

4th day–100 ml.

After fourth day the internal oleation continued to achieve Samyak Snehyan. Lower age group received lower dose.

External Oleation

Sesame oil was applies over the trunk and extremities for external oleation.

Sudation

After Samayak Snehyan and Sarvang Abhyang medicated steam bath (Swedan) was given to widen the channels and eliminate the toxins of the body.

Vaman (Emesis)

Purv Karm

Patients were given sesame oil for three days in increasing order with initial dose of 30ml. The stool become oily. Kaphgenic diet was given to aggrevate, kaph in the system.

A day before Vaman patients were given oil massage and fomentation. Next morning vaman is done with Madan Phal Kalp*.

**Madan Phal Preparation*: Add 10 gm of Madan phal and 10 gm of pippli to 200 ml of Mulathi Kwath. This decoction is kept throughout the night. Add 10 gms of sendhev and 20 gms of Honey to it in the morning. This mixture is Madan Phal Kalp.

Vamari Procedure: At morning patients were asked to drink milk full stomach and then given Madan Phal kalp. Vomiting was induced and continued till pittant was achieved.

Paschyat Karm

Complete rest and fasting.

Sansarjan Karm: Peya, Velapi, Yush or meat soup is given to the patient.

Virechan: Virechan was done after 15 days. Both external and internal oleation was done regularly for three days. Snehpan was given in this order

1st day–150 ml.

2nd day–100 ml.

3rd day–50 ml.

Virechan Kalp* was used to remove the dosh of bowl till Kaphant was achieved.

*Virechan Kalp Preparation

Kutki–20 gm.

Nishoth–20 gm.

Choti Harer–20 gm.

Make Kwath of this mixture in 200 ml of water. Add 20 ml of castor oil and give to the patient empty stomach.

After Virechan Sansarjan Karm was done accordingly.

Following Instructions–were given to the patients that they:

1. Should avoid the factors, places, business that causes Asthma.
2. Should avoid common cold, cold drinks and moist places.
3. Must go for daily morning walk, do yoga exercises (Surya Namaskar and Pranayam).
4. Must go to sleep in time at night.
5. Should avoid mental tension.
6. Must brush teeth every morning after every meal and have good hygiene life.
7. Must avoid Tobacoo, wine and smoking habits.
8. Must avoid over eating and take light dinner one hour before going to bed.
9. Should not over load house with furniture and carpets.
10. Should keep room ventilated and use exhaust fan in the kitchen.
11. Should avoid air conditioner, cooler and direct air of fan.
12. Must avoid perfumes, aggarbatti, mosquito repellents that aggrevets attack.
13. Must not over exercise, over do sex, over do work, eat rough food, take excess emesis and laxative and suppress toilet urge.
14. Must drink boiled water in excess.
15. Must avoid those medicines which aggravates asthmatic symptoms.

16. Patients of Asthma children were advised to inform the schools teacher to keep their ward out of aggravating activities.

Advise Given for

What to Eat?

Hot soup of Bengal gram, Gram flour mixed with wheat flour, Garlic, Black pepper, Asafoetida, Clove, Basil leaves, Long pepper, Mint leaves, Papaya, Carrot, Carrot juice, Radish, Apple, Black resin, fig, Dates, Almond, Barley flour, Honey, Spinach, Rock salt, Cumin seeds, Lemon Grass Tea.

What Not to Eat?

Beans, Pea, Excess pulses, Cheese, Banana, Oranges, Water melon, Curd, Rice, Oily food, Bread, Jam, Pickels.

Medicines Used

Shwas kas Chintamani Ras, Shwas Kutar Ras, Sitopladi Churn, Talisadi Churn, Vasavakha, Chawanprash.

Krimi Mudgar Ras was given as antihelminthic.

Results

The results show remarkable changes in all the patients. The panchkarma reestablished the immunity of the bio-system. Hence, the change in the clinical picture were outstanding. The absolute eosinophyll count was elevated in 90 per cent of cases. After panchkarma and treatment 75 per cent showed normal. The HB was shown below the normal level in 35 per cent cases. Most of them were children and females. A course of Antihelminth was given to intestinal infestation cases prior to panchkarma. The medication was given for three month. There was no relapse of wheezing after three month in 82 cases, 12 cases had wheezing once or twice during the course 10 cases did not respond well and six cases discontinued:

Total cases of Tamak Shwas–120

Cured–Excellent–92

Cured–Good–12

Poor–10

Discontinued–No result–6

Chapter 11

Medicinal Plants of Rigveda

Deepika Chauhan, Navneet and Prabhat
Department of Botany and Microbiology, Gurukula Kangri University, Haridwar – 249 404, India

ABSTRACT

Vedas are the light house for the entire humanity. The light of the Vedas is the foundation of world. Vedas promote universal brotherhood, human welfare and universal prosperity. Vedas have a wider spectrum of knowledge embedded in them, as they can rightly be declared to be the true repositories of all eternal and true knowledge. To say that the Vedas contain only the spiritual and religious material, will be the travesty of truth. From the time immemorial, Vedas have been supposed to be treasure-house of all knowledge and were declared as the only source head of every thought and action. Maharishi Dayananda, the greatest vedic scholar of this age, wrote in most unambiguous terms. "Vedas are the respositories of all true knowledge".

Our ancient medical system which is still in vogue as ayurvedic system, originated and developed from Rigveda and many facts of life and culture, education and bearing, economy and polity as well as custom and tradition have roots in Rigveda. According to Vedas the causative agents of disease are organisms and poisons.The germs, organisms and insects are five types, *i.e.* visible (drasta), invisible (adrasta), creeping insects (kururu), living in beds etc. (algandu) and moving fast (salune). There are two types of germs: Durnama and Sunama. Durnama cause disease hence must be destroyed. Sunama nourish the body, hence must live there. Rigveda widely deals with the medicine and herbs, their healing properties and their importance. Herbs are the important source of curing disease. On the basis of their healing properties and their importance. Medicines were prepared from the extract of these herbs. The extracts of herbs have been described as the source of longevity. In Rigveda hundreds of herbs were used as medicine.

Introduction

Popular tradition says that there are four Vedas–the Rig, the Yajur, the Sama and the Atharveda. Oodox opinion limits the number to the first three. The Atharveda has little common with the other and the language indicates a latter era. These Vedas represents the several schools of vedic thoughts founded respectively by paila, vaisampayana, jaimini and sumanta. Each veda consist of two parts, the mantra and the brahmana. The first consists of the second is a collection of rules prescribing the method and plan of the various rituals and ceremonies at which the mantras are to be recited, together with illustrative remarks explaining the origin and purpose of each rite. Of the

Samhitas the most copious is Rigveda. The Yajur veda deals largely with sacrificial liturgy.

The Rigveda form the full content of the worship of the Vedas and that a study of that veda will help the incurring student to have a fair knowledge of the social and religious institutions. The rigveda samhita consist of the 1017 hymns of different lengths they were apparently enchanted by several rishis at different sacrificial rites and during other ceremonies. Vedic scholar classify hymns in two different ways. One arrangement divides them into eight khandas or Ashtakas and each Ashtakas into eight adhyas or chapters. The other plan divides the suktas or hymns into ten mandalas or cycles. The foundation stone that India contributed to civilization, the Vedas is said to embody the regulations, the laws of the universe as seen by the gifted poet, prophets, or seers the sis, to be the Indians. The authority of the Vedas is supreme and final point the Vedas was given to man at the earliest stage, when the biological species was sufficiently evolved to receive the divine inspiration it continued to inspire human literature for millenniums of years. In India most ancient human's literature that we possess now is that of the books known as the Brahmanas, but they were also written thousands of years after the divine revolution. These Brahmanas all without exception, accept the authority of Vedas.

The Indian tradition tells us the Vedas originally excited as a single unit, and that it was only latter on that they were classify into sakhas for sacrificial purposes by vyasas. Diligent researches in carefull scrutinizes have led the scholars and the critics of the rigvedas to found the ostensible conclusion that the samhitas is a religious work that is historical work and so on.

Every Hindu believes that his religious practices and rites are based upon the Vedas. The Vedas relate to the worship of the Devas. This worship comprehends offerings, prayers and praises. The offering to the Vedas consisted of oblation and liberation: Ghee poured on the fire, and Juice of the soma plant. The hymns recited the glories of the Deva invoked, and describe that power, the goodness and even the personal beauty of the Deva addressed. They also rehearse the past bounties and explits of the Devas. The Devas are implored to bestow blessings on the man who has instituted the ceremony in which these hymns are recited. The blessings prayed, for the most part, of the a temporal nature wealth of cattle and horses, and protection against enemies. It is also assured that the Devas derive much benefits from the offerings made to them and that the praises addressed to them augment their power for good.

The Vedas are the permeable source of knowledge, which paved the way for the advent to world culture and world civilization. The significance of the Vedas is discernible in the entire Indian heritage. The Vedas are the treasures of knowledge and the origin of Dharma. The extension of the basic knowledge emanated from the Vedas and they are the light house for entire humanity. The light of the Vedas promotes universal brotherhood, human welfare and universal prosperity. The Vedas have been at the root of cultural and social consciousness. The study and analysis of Vedas have shaped various cultures. The Vedas have refined not only the Indian culture but also the world culture. The west has benefited from the study of the Vedas as much as India.

Description of Plant

Sigru (*Moringa oleifera*)

आवदिन्द्रं यमुना तृत्सवश्रव प्रात्र भेदं सर्वताता मुषायत् ।
आजासश्रव षिग्रवो यक्षवश्रव बलिं शीर्षाणिं जभ्रुरश्व्यानि ॥

RV; 7.18.19

Sigru is a small or medium sized tree and attains the height of about 10m. It is found wild in the sub Himalayan tract and is also cultivated throughout India. Root, bark, fruit, flower and seeds are used as medicine.

This is a green and woody plant. This plant bears a white yellowish flowers.

Phytochemistry

Preliminary chemical investigation of *M. oleifera* bark revealed the presence of steroids and terpenes and absence of alkaloids, saponin, tannins and mucilage. The hexane extract of the bark yielded a triterpenoid–bayrenol *Moringa oleifera* leaves on ethanoic extraction yielded a number of amino acids, viz, aspartic acid, glutamic acid serine, glycine and, theonine, α–alanine, valine, leucine iso-leusine, histidine, lysine, arginine, phenylaneine, tryptophan, cystine and methionine. The ether extract of leaves yielded α and β carotene. Latter nine amino acids in the flower, eight in the fruits and seven each in the protein hydrolysate of flower and fruits of *M. oleifera*. They were identified as alanine, arginine, glutamic acid, glycine, cerine, threonine and valine. These amino acids were common in all the parts tested, where as aspartic acid was present in the flower as well as the fruits and lycine occurred only in the flower. The flower contain both sucrose and D–Glucose where as the fruits showed the presence of sucrose only.

Pharmacology

The roots are carminative and stomachic, abortiacient, cardiac tonic and also use in paralytic conditions and intermittent fever. They are also useful as rubefacient, in spasmodic affections of the bowels, hysteria and flatulence as well as in epilepsy. Root bark is used as fermentation to relive spam. Bark is considered to be an abortifacient. Seed oil is applied extremely in rheumatism. Leaves are emetic and their juice with black peppers is used in headache. The poultice of leaves is used in reducing glandular swellings.

Durva *(Cynadon dactylon)*

यं त्वमग्ने समदहतस्तमु निर्वापया: ।

कियाम्ब्वात्र रोहतु पाकदूर्वा व्यल्कशा ।।

RV; 10.16.13

Description

It is perennial and creeping herb with underground rhizome. Culms are decumbent–ascending and nodes are glabrous. Leaves are linear sub late and scabrid on the upper surface margin. Ligules are minute, scarious, erose and ciliate rim. The sheaths are composes, keeled, and glabrous exept hairy throat. Spikes are 2–4 and 1.5–3.0 cm × 0.1–2 cm spikelets are 0.02 cm × 0.1 cm lower glume is linear lancelets, acute, 1 nerved and 0.1 cm long. Upper glume is about 0.1 cm long. Lemmas are 3 nerve, bidentate, mucronate and ciliate on the keel in the upper half. Pleasures 2–keeled and 0.1–0.2 cm long. Stamens are 3 grains oblong and free within the glumes. Flowering is during July–September and fruiting October–December.

Phytochemistry

No information is available.

Pharmacology

The decoction of its root is diuretic and is used in dropsy and in secondary syphilis. An infusion of the root is used for stopping bleeding from piles and crushed roots mixed with curd used in chronic gleet. The juice of the plant is said to be astringent and is used externally to fresh cuts and wounds and internally as diuretic. It is used in dropsy and anasarca, hysteria, epilepsy, insanity, in chronic diarrhoea, dysentery.

Kusha *(Desmostachya bipinnata)*

शरासः कुशरासो दर्भासः सैर्या उत ।
मौञ्ज अदृष्टा बैरिणा चमत बमदज साकं न्यलिप्सत ॥

RV; 1.191.3

Description

It is tufted and perennial grasses with a thick root stock, culums are erect and nodes are glabrous. The leaves are liner, narrowed into a filiform tip and 0.1-0.3 cm broad.The sheaths are glabrous with hairy throut.The panicles are 45.0 cm, 1.0-2.0 cm. The spikes are crowded and 1.0-3 cm. The spikelets are purple brown, biseriata and 3-4 flowered. The lower glume is keeled, mucronate, 1-neved and 0.5-0.07 cm long and the upper glume is 0.1 cm long. The lemmas are subacute with scabrid keeled, and 3 nerved. The paleas are 0.13 cm long stamens are 3 and the anthers are 0.08-0.1 cm long Grains are 0.05-0.06 cm long, obliquely ovoid, trigonous and laterally compressed.

Phytochemistry

The leaf culms yield pectose, lignin, cellulose and ash.

Pharmacology

The roots are bitter, sweet, cooling diuretic, emollient, galactagogue and astringent and are used in asthma, jaundice, vitated conditions of pitta and hyperdipsia. The culms are, diuretic, stimulant and are used in diarrhoea, dysentery, leucorrhoea, skin diseases, stones, memorrhagia and thirst.

Vamsa (*Bambusa arudinacea* Roxb)

ओचित्सरवायं सरव्या वव त्यां तिरः पुरु चिदर्णवं जगन्वान् ।
थ्पतुर्नपातमा दधीत वेघा अधि क्षमि प्रतरं दीघ्यानः ॥

RV; 1.10.1

Description

It is a tall bamboo with crowded culms arising from branching roots stock. Culms-sheath are rounded at apex and hairy with dark-brown hairs on the back and glabrous within.The leaves are linear or linear-lenceolate and glabrous or hairy beneath.The inflorescence is an enormous panicle, often comprising of the whole culm. The spikletes are lanceolate and acute. Grains are ending in a shoret beack and about 0.5-0.8 cm long.

Phytochemistry

The roots contain cyanyenetic glucoside, benzoic acid, resin and waxes. Besides, cholin, betain and enzymes have also been reported from the plant.

Pharmacology

The leaves are emmenagogue and are used in haematemesis. Dastur (1962), stated that a decoction of its leaves is given to India after childbirth and as anthelmitic, these are particularly useful for threadworm. The juice of leaves with aromatics is given in blood, vomiting and an infusion of the leaves given internally for gonorrhoea.

Aratu *(Oroxylum indicum)*

अयं दशस्यन्नर्येभिरस्य दस्मो देवेभिर्वरुणो न मायी ।
अयं कनीन ऋतुपा अवेधमिमीताररु यातुष्पात् ॥

RV; 8.46.27

Description

A small to medium sized deciduous tree, grows throughout greater part of India at, 200 m except in western drier areas.

Phytochemistry

Root bark, stem bark, fruits and seeds is used.

The ethanolic extract of *O. indicum* leaves gave baicalein and scutellarein, from the ether fraction, a flavone glycoside, identified as baicalein-6-glucuronide, from the ethylacetate fraction, and two glucuronides identified as scutellarein-7-glucuronide acid baicalein-7-glucuronide from the aqueous mother liquor. The defatted leaves of *O. indicum* on extraction with choloroform yielded, a gummy solid yielding an anthraquinone, aloe–emdin.

The ethanolic extract of the stem bark of *O. indicum* on fractionation yielded oroxylin-A from the benzoic extractive; oroxylin-A, baicalein and scutellarein from ether extractive and scutellarein-7-rutinosid from the ethylacetate fraction. Chrysin and baicalein-7-glucronide also occurred in the mother liquor of ether and ethylacetate fraction.

Pharmacology

The decoction of *O. indicum* bark showed good diuretic activity in rats, comparing favourably with potassium acetate and being more potent than urea. The ethanolic extract of the fruits of *O. indicum* showed spasmogenic action on isolated guinea pig ileum, whereas the root and stem as well as the stem bark extracts had no such effect. The plant was devoid of antibacterial, antifungal, antiprotozol, anthelmintic, antiviral hypoglycaemic and anticancer activities. It has no effect on CNS and CVS.

Kimsuka *(Butea monosperma)*

सुकिंशुकं शल्मलिं विरूपं हिरण्यवर्णं सुवृतं सुचक्रम् ।
आ रोह सूर्ये अमृतस्य लोकं स्योनं पत्ये वहतुं कृणुष्व ॥

RV; 10.85.20

Description

It is a moderate sized deciduous tree upto 15 cm high and 1.5-1.8m girth. The bark is fibrous, bluish-grey or light brown and exuding a ruby red vitreous gum. The leaves are pinnately 3-foliate, large, unequal and 10.2-20.4 cm. The flowers are 3.8-5.0 cm long and orange-red and are fasicled on rigid axillary and terminal racemes.The pods are silvery-white and broad. The seeds are flat, elliptic reddish grey and 3.2 cm across. Flowering is in February-March and fruiting during April-May.

Phytochemistry

The flowers contain butein and its 7-glucoside and 3β-D-glucoside, isomonopermoside, coreopsin, sulphurein, palastrin, butein and isobutein. The gum from bark contain leucocyanidin and its tetramer (procyanidin), riboflavin and thiamine. Glycine, a glycoside and an aromatic hydroxy compound have been separated from the roots of the plant unsponifiable matter of seed oil contains α-amyrin, β-sitosterol and its glucosides.The fatty acid composition of the seed oil comprises of myristic, palmitic, stearic, arachidic, behenic, lignoceric, olic, linleic and linoleic acids. The seeds contain palasonic, aleuritic and jalaric acid, laccijaric acid and its derivatives, cantharic n-heneicsonic acid and nonospermin.

Pharmacology

The seeds are anthelmintic, acid, bitter, aperient and rubefacient. The seeds are used in flatatulence and piles. A decoction of seeds is given in gravel and paste of powdered seed with lemon juice is applied in herpes and as a cure of ring worms and also for cooling effect. Fine powder of seeds along with *Acorus calamus* rhizome or mixed with juice of *Cyperus rotundus* rhizomes is used as a cure for delirium.The flowers are diuretic, depurative, astringent and aphrodisid.

Haridra or Haridrava *(Pinus deodara)*

शुकेषु मे हरिमाणं रोपणाकासु दध्मसि ।
अथो हारिद्रवेषु मे हरिमाणं नि दध्मसि ॥

RV; 1.50.12

The generic name Pinus has been derived from Greek word pinos, used by Theophrastus for a pine tree.

Description

It is large tree with systematical branches high upon the trunk and forming a round head of light foliage and reaching up to 30 m in height. Normally, it is evergreen but becomes completely or partially deciduous in dry season. The bark is dark grey and deeply fissured. The leaves are 20-30 cm long, arranged in form of cones which are 1.5 cm long. Female cones are 10.0–20.0 cm × 7.5-12.0 cm, ovoid and are solitary or 2-5 together and woody. The seeds without wings are 0.7-1.3 cm × 0.5-0.6 cm and winged; wings are membranous and long.

The cones formation is started in January next year during June–July its cones become old and in next summer, burst and seeds are shed out. About 26 months are spared to complete the whole process. The dry cones remain long on the tree.

Phytochemistry

The plant contains α- and β-Pinene and careen. These needles of plants are good source of vitamin C and E and carotenes. The heart wood contains stilvene and flavonoids namely pinosylvin, pinocemvrin and pinovanksin.

Pharmacology

The wood is stimulant, diaphoretice, and is useful in the burning of the body, cough, fainting and ulceration. The wood is said to be beneficial in snake-bite and scorpion-stings also. The oleoresin is considered to by anodyne and diuretic and is beneficial in coryza, and oedema. This is adviced to be given in the doses of 1.8–5.4 gm four times daily in gonorrhoea. It is expectorant and useful in chronic bronchitis and is specially recommended in gangrene of lungs, also given as carminative in flatulent colic and to arrest minor hemorrhages in tooth socket and nose. Externally, it is used as a ruvefacient in rheumatic affection and for deep seated inflammation, especially of abdomen and applied as a plaster to be bubos and absence for suppuration.

Muja (*Saccharum munja*)

वर्धी वृत्रं मरुत इन्द्रियेण स्वेन भामेन तविषो वभृवान् ।
अहमेता मनवे विन्द्रः सुगाा अपाकर वज्रबाहु ॥

RV; 1.161.8

It is a tall perennial grass with erect culms. The leaves are linear, somewhat glaucous beneath, scabride on the margin and upto 2 cm broad. The pennical is dense and wide, while villous upto 100 cm long with whorled branches. Sessile spikelets are lanceolate, acute, 0.5 cm long and 2–nerved. The pedicelled spikelets are similar to sessile spikelets flowering and fruiting is during October–January. Stamens and roots are used.

Phytochemistry

The stem is considered as refrigerant and aphrodisiac. These are useful in burning sensation, blood problems, thirst, erysipelas and urinary complaints. The roots are used as diuretic and demulcent.

Madhuka or Mahuva (*Madhuka indika*)

सूर्ये विषमा सजामि तिं सुरावतो गृहे ।
सो चित्रु न मराति नो वयं मरामारे
अस्ययोजनं हरिष्ठा मधु त्वा मधुला चंकार ॥

RV; 1.192.10-13

Description

It is a large deciduous tree with about 17m. height. The bark is grey or blackish with shallow wrinkle and vertical cracks. Young branches, leaves and petioles are pubescent or tomentose. The leaves are clustered at the ends of branches, 12.5-17.5 cm × 7.5-10.0 cm, elliptic or oblong-elliptic and shortly acuminate base. The flowers are many, at the ends of the branches and are borne on droping pedicels. The calyx is coriaceous and densely rusty-tomentose. The corolla is yellowish-white and early caducous. Stamens are 20–30 and anthers are hispid with stiff hairs. The fruits are ovoid, fleshy and green berries and about 2.5-5.0 cm long. The seeds are 1-4. Flowering is during April–May and fruiting in June–July.

Phytochemistry

Isolated leucodelphindin from the bark of the plant. The fruits contain vitamin A and C, ethylcinnamate, sesquiterpene alcohol, α-terpenol, 3β-monocaprylic ester of erythrodiol and 3β-capryloxy oleanolic acid and α and β-amyrin. The seed-oil has arachidic, linoleic, olic, myristic, palmitic and steric acid.

The flower contain L-arabinose, D-galactose, glucose, D-glucuronin acid, fructose, maltose, L-rhamnose, D-xylose, biotin, folic acid, isositol, niacin, pantothenic and riboflavin, thiannin, amylase, catalase, emulsion, invertase, maltase, oxidase, malic acid and sussinic acid, anthocyanin, betaine acid and protein.

Pharmacology

The seeds are laxative and are used in piles and constipation. The gummy juice of the seed is applied in rheumatism and skin-diseases. The residual cake mowrah meal, obtain after the extraction of the oil from the seeds is said to be used as fish poison and as worm-killer for lawns. The decoction of the bark is also used as astringent, emollient, hypoglycaemic and tonic and their powder is used in bleeding gums, stomachache, tonsilitis and diabetes.

Besides, the stem-bark also possesses some insecticidal properties.

Asvavati, Udojasa, Urjayanti (*Ficus religiosa*)

असबत्थे वो निषदनं पर्णे वो वसतिष्कृता ।
गोभाज इत्किलासथयत्सनवथ पूरुषम् ॥

RRV; 10.97.7

Description

It is a large or medium-sized deciduous tree with speading branches of about 10-12m thick. Bark is grey with brownish specks, smooth and 1.3 cm thick. Trunks are irregularly shaped. The leaves are alternate, 10.0–17.5 cm × 7.5–12.5 cm, broadly ovate or round, caudate and long petioled. Male flowers are very few and sessile, sepals 3, stamen 1 and filament short Female and gall flowers, sepals 5, style short and lateral. Fruits are sessile in axillary pairs, depressed-globose, 1.3 cm across and dark purple when ripe.

Flower is during summer and fruiting in rainy season.

Phytochemistry

The bark contain β-sitosteryl-d-glucoside and vitamin K, n-octacosanol, methyloleanolate, lenosterol, stigmasterol and lupin-3 one have been reported from its stem bark.

Pharmacology

According to Chopra *et al.* (1956), the bark is astringent and is used in gonorrhoea. Pulverised bark is applied externally on unhealthy ulcer and wounds to promote granulation and found very efficaceous when rubbed with honey to apthous sores of children. The dried bark in powdered form is used in and fistula and in the form of a

Table 11.1

Name of the Vedic Plant	Botanical Name of the Vedic Plant	Family of the Vedic Plant	References
ASVAVATI,UDOJASA,URJAYANTI	*Ficus religiosa*	Moraceae	RV; 10.97.7
JIVANTI	*Leptadenia reticulata*	Asclepiadaceae	RV; 5.78.9
VISANAKA	*Gymnema sylvestre*	Asclepiadaceae	RV; 6.16.20 RV; 9.96.8
SIGRU	*Moringa oleifera*	Moringaceae	RV; 7.18.19
HARIDRA(HALDI)	*Curcuma longa*	Zingiberaceae	RV; 1.50.11-12
ARATU/ARADU			
ARALU	*Oroxylum indicum*	Bignoniaceae	RV; 8.46.27
ASVATTHA	*Ficus religiosa*	Moraceae	RV; 1.138.8 RV; 10.97.5 RV; 1.35.8 RV; 1.164.4
UDUMBARA	*Ficus glomerata*	Moraceae	RV; 10.14.12
KARUNJA	*Pongamia glabra*	Leguminacae	RV; 1.53.8 RV; 10.48.8
KARSMARYA or KASMARYA	*Gmelina arbora*	Verbanaceae	RV; 6.48.1-7
KIMSUKA	*Butea monosperma*	Leguminaceae	RV; 10.85.20

Contd...

Table 11.1–Contd...

Name of the Vedic Plant	Botanical Name of the Vedic Plant	Family of the Vedic Plant	References
KHADIRA	*Acacia catechu*	Leguminaceae	RV; 3.18.19 RV; 3.15.19 RV; 3.53.19
PALASA	*Butea frandosa*	Leguminaceae	RV; 10.97.5 RV; 4.2.7-4
MADHUKA (MAHUVA)	*Madhuka indica*	Sapotaceae	RV; 1.191.10-13
VIBHITAKA or VIBHIDAKA	*Terminalia bellerica*	Combretaceae	RV; 7.86.6 RV; 10.34.1
SALMALI	*Bombax ceiba*	Bombacaceae	RV; 7.50.3 RV; 10.85.20 RV; 3.53.22
SIMSAPA	*Delbergia sisso*	Leguminaceae	RV; 3.53.19 RV; 3.15.9
HARIDRA or HARIDRAVA	*Pinus deodara*	Pinaceae	RV; 1.50.12
AVAKA	*Blyxa octandra*	Hydracharitaceao	RV; 10.68.5
URVARU (KHAIR)	*Cucumis sativus*	Cucurbitacae	RV; 7.59.12

Contd...

Table 11.1–Contd...

Name of the Vedic Plant	*Botanical Name of the Vedic Plant*	*Family of the Vedic Plant*	*References*
PUDARIKA	*Nelumbo nucifera*	Nympheaceae	RV; 10.142.8 RV; 10.107.16 RV; 7.33.11 RV; 8.72.11 RV; 6.16.13
MADHUVATI	*Vitis vinifera*	Vitaceae	RV; 10.16.3
ARJUNA	*Terminalia arjuna*	Combretaceae	RV; 1.122.5 RV; 3.39.2 RV; 7.55.2
KASA	*Sacchraum spontaneum*	Gramineae	RV; 10.100.10
KUSA	*Desmostachya bipinnata*	Gramineae	RV; 1.191.3
DURVA	*Cynadon dactylon*	Gramineae	RV; 10.16.13 RV; 10.134.5 RV; 10.142.8
BHANGA	*Cannabis sativa*	Cannabiaceae	RV; 9.61.13
MUNJA	*Sacchrum munja*	Gramineae	RV; 1.161.8 RV; 1.191.3
VAMSA	*Bambusa arundinadea*	Gramineae	RV; 1.10.1

Contd...

Table 11.1–Contd...

Name of the Vedic Plant	*Botanical Name of the Vedic Plant*	*Family of the Vedic Plant*	*References*
YUVA	*Hordeum vulgare*	Gramineae	Rv; 1.23.15 RV; 1.66.3 Rv; 1.117.21 RV; 1.44.11 RV; 1.135.8 RV; 1.176.2 RV; 2.5.6

paste, as an absorbent in inflammatory swelling.Tender and fresh leaves are beneficial when used alongwith butter fat to cover the inflammatory ulcers. The oil medicated with its leaves is used as ear drops in ear ache. The leaves and its twigs are also considered as laxative.The seeds are laxative and in powder form these are given for three days during menses as to sterilized women. Besides, various parts of the plant are used in otitis media, suppurativa, mouth sores, atrophy, emaciation or cachexy, rheumatism, smallpox, carbuncle, mucus in urine, spermatorrhoea, gravel, cholera and rinderpest.

Khadera (*Acacia catechu*)

अभि व्ययस्व खदिरस्य सारमोजोधेहि स्पन्दने शिंपायाम् ।
अक्ष वीड्वो वीड्वयस्व मायामादस्मादव जीहिपो नः ॥

RV; 3.18.19

The generic name *Acacia catechu* has been adopted from Greek word Akis a sharp paint, reffering to the thorns of the plant.

Description

It is moderate-sized tree with thorny branches. Bark is rough, dark grey or grayish-brown and about 1.2 cm thick exporting in long narrow strips. The leaves are 10.0-17.5 cm long, pinnate with a pairs of recurves pirckles at base of rachis and pinnae 40-80, leaflets are 60-100 small and ligulate. Flowers are pale-yellow in axillary cylindrical spikes. The pods are thin, glabrous, lustrous, straight, star-shaped, dark brown and orbicular.

Flowering is in rainy season and fruiting during November–January.

Phytochemistry

Catechu contain 2-12 per cent catechins 25-23 per cent phlobatannin, 20-30 per cent gummy matter, quercitrin and querchitin. The Acacia tree has epicatechin that is distinct from catechin in gum gambhir. Epicatehin from white acellular crystals which are soluble in hot water and alcohol and given a green colour with ferric salts. Catechutannic acid is an amorphous, phlobatannin, which forms epicatechin by loss of the elements of water, it readily yields the phlobouphene catechu–red.

Pharmacology

A flavonoid from the plant was found to have significant anti-inflammatory effect. No significant neuropharmalogical effects were seen. Alkaloids show mild hypotensive effects. The astringent principles of the plant have a protein precipitating activity on mucosal surfaces and in wounds and ulcers. Catechu is widely used as a component of the beetel leaf chewed in India. It is used for the local treatment of otitis and otorrhoea. It is also useful indental, oral, throut and tonsillar infections, and as an astringent for reducing oozine ulcers and wounds. The extract in also indermatoses-locally systematically.

Karanja (*Pongamia pinnata*)

त्वं करञ्जमुत पर्णयं वधीस्तेजि ठयातिथिग्वस्य वर्तनी ।
त्वं शता वृंदस्याभिनत्पुरोऽनानुदः परिषूता ऋजिना ॥

RV; 1.53.8

Pongamia pinnata is known as karanja in Sanskrit. Two species of Karanja *viz.*, urkara karanja (*P. glabra*), kanta-karanja or cirivivah karanja (*P. pinnata*) have been found in India. The plant are common throughout India. They are planted along road side as an avenue tree and also distributed in Eastern Asia, Himalaya, Sri Lanka, Burma, Malaya, Northern Australia and Polynesia.

Description

P. pinnata bark is grayish, green or brown, smooth and covered with tubercles, leaves, imparipinnate, leaflets 5-7, ovate or elliptic, flower, lilauce, or white tinged with pink or violet, fragrant in axillary racemes, pods compressed woody, indehiscent, yellowish grey when ripe, varying in size and shape, elliptic to obliquely, oblong 4.0 -5.0 cm broad with a short curved beak, seed usually 1, rarely 2, elliptical or reniform, 1.7–2.0 cm long and 1.2–1.8 cm broad wrinkled with reddish, brown leathery testa. The harvest season extends in generally obtained from November–December to May–June. The pods are collected and the shells removed by hand.

Phytochemistry

The oil resembles ground nut oil in composition. The fatty acid composition of the oil shows the following ranges of values: palmitic, 3.7-7.9; stearic, 2.4-8.9; aracihidic, 2.2-4.7, behenic, 4.2-5.3; legnoceric, 1.1-3.5, oleic, 44.5-71.3, levolic, 10.8-18.3 and eicoenoic, 9.5-12.4 per cent and traces of docorrenoic and tetracosemic acids. The un-saponifible matter contain β-sitosterol. Karanjin and ponganol compounds isolated from *P. pinnata*. Karanj is highly toxic to fish, pong mol exhibit comparatively mild toxicity. The flowers contain an aliphatic waxy matter, free kaempferol, pongamin, γ–site sterol glucoside, guercetin, negoglobrin and glabrosaponin. The stem bark contains two closely related derivatives, kananjin and dimethoxy karanj in feebly toxic to fish. The root bark from Australia been reported to contain Karanj and pongapin and smaller amount of two linear furamo flavones, pinnata and gumatin which are isomeric with karanjin and pongupin respectively. The roots admixture part extract contain anticancer alkaloid as pacitaxol, fluorophenylanine.Vinblastin sulphate and vincristin sulphate, teniposide and octoporide derivative compounds.

Pharmacology

In Ayurveda, karanja in highly valued for the treatment of many diseases. It is applied in scabies, herpe's, leucoderma, dyspepsia with sluggish liver. The galactaggue juice of leaves is prescribed in flat ulcers, dyspepsia, diarrhoea. Cough and used in leprosy and gonorrhoea. Roots juice is used for cleaning foul ulcers, gonorrohoea and flat ulcers sores, decoction of fresh bark is used in beriberi. The decoction of flowers juice used for diabetes. The seed are also used to treat painful, rheumatic joints, skin disease leprous sores. Root admixture extract found exclusive anti-cancer compounds.

Karanj has been used extensively by our Rishis and practioners of Ayurveda since time immemorial.

Madhuvati (*Vitis vinifera*)

अपो वा गच्छयदि तत्र ते हितमोषधीषु
प्रति तिष्ठा शरीरै : ।
अजो भागस्तपसा तं तपस्व तं ते शोचिस्तपतु
तं ते अर्चि ॥

RV; 10.16.3

Description

It is a large woody climber bitid tendrils. The leaves are globorous above, clothed beneath with grey deciduous tomentum, suborbiculear, cordate and more or less deeply 5-lobed. The flowers are pentamerous and green and are borne in umbel-like cymes, which form large pyramidal compound panicles. The fruits are subglobose berries with 1-5 seed. But the fruits realy come to perfection due to heavy rainfall which usually takes place before these have properly ripened.

Phytochemistry

The mature fruits contain malic, tartaric acid, cemic acid, which the oxalic acid has been reported from its unripe fruits.

Pharmacology

Grapes, juice, sap, leaves, dried fruits and ashes of the wood are used. The grapes are demulcent, laxative, refrigerant, stomachic, diuretic and cooling. These are considered very useful in chronictic and bronchitis, heart-disease, brights disease and gout. The juice of the unripe grapes is astringent and is used in throat affection. Straind grape juice, one tea spoonful is given to children for constipation. The juice is also good for thrush in children and that of sour grapes is useful for bruise and sprains the sap of the young branches. The leaves are astringent and are used in diarrhoea. Dried fruits, known as Munakka are cooling demulcent, sweet, laxative and stomachic.

Kasa *(Saccharum spontaneum)*

यव्दाग्वदन्तेविचेतनानि राष्ट्री देवनां निषसाद मन्द्रा ।
चतस्त्र ऊर्ज दुदुहे पयांसि क्क स्विदस्याः परमं जगाम ।।

RV; 10.100.10

Description

It is perennial gregarious grass with glaborous and erect culms. The leaves are linear-filiform, glaucous beneath, often reduced to midrib, scabrid on the margin and 0.1-0.4 cm broad. The sheaths are auriculate and glabrous except hairy throat. Pedicels are ciliate and 2-0.3 cm long sessile spikelets are liner-lanceolate and 0.3–0.4 cm × 0.04.005 cm flowering and fruiting is during September-December.

Phytochemistry

The plant has been reported to contain calcium oxalate.

Pharmacology

The root and whole plant is used. The roots are diuretic and a decoction of roots with that of Gokshra and Mishri is given to remove urinary bladder calculi. The plant is considered as laxative and aphrodisiac. An extract of the plant is given in burning sensation, phthisis, blood disease, vesical calculi, bilousness and haemorrhagic diathesis.

Bhanga (*Cannabis sativa*)

उपो पु जातमप्तुरं गोभिर्भं परिष्कृतम् ।
इन्दुं देवा अयासिट्टः ॥

RV; 9.61.13

Description

It is a tall annual herb about 1.2-4.9m high with angular stem. The leaves are palmate, alternate or lower one opposite and 5.0-0.20.0 cm long, the lobes of the upper leaves are 1-5 and in lower 5-11, liner lanceolate, sharpely toothed, long-pointed and narrowed at base. The flowers are small, greenish and unisexual. The males are born in long dropping panicles and female in short axillary spikes.

The achenes are 3 cm aross, ovate and flat and are enclosed in persistent perianth. Flowering and fruiting is during March–May.

Phytochemistry

The plant contains cannabinol, tetrahydrocannabinol, cannabidiol, cannabichromene, 1-dehydrotetrahydro-cannabinal and acid other phenolic compounds along with eugenol, guaicol-sequiterpenes, hydrocarbons, piperidine, amino acid prenylated and c-glycosylflavonoids.

Pharmacology

The seed, leaves, dried flowering or fruiting tops of the female plant and resinous exudates are used for medicinal purposes.

The plant is considered as a tonic analysic and antiseptic and is useful in gonorrhoea, menorrhagia, diarrhoea, holera, hydrophobia, tetanus and rheumatism. The leaves are used in ear troubles and their juice is upplied on cuts after mixing with sugar. The juice of leaves is also used to destroy worm and vermin. The crushed leaves are applied on skin in skin diseases. The chronic use of cannabis useful in patients of diabetic hypertension the leaves are also used as snuff and are given internally about 5 gm per day to relieve pain and swelling.

Pundarika (*Nelumbo nucifera*)

अभ्यारमिदद्रयो निषित्कं पुघु । अवतस्य विसर्जने ॥

RV; 10.107.16

Description

It is an attractive perennial herb with creeping rhizome. The leaves are orbicular, glaucous, floating, pettate and 60-

90 cm in diameter, petiole is very long and smooth or pickly. Flowers are solitary, bisexual, regular, large, rosy, white or rarely yellow and 10.2-25.4 cm across. Sepals are 4-5 and caducous. Petals are many seriate, caducous. Stamens are many-seriate carpels are irregularly scattered and ovules 1-2 fruits are torus, spongy, rop-shaped and 5.0-10.0 cm in diameter. Seeds are elongated, spherical, smooth, black and exalbuminous.

Phytochemistry

The plant contains a number of alkaloids, roemerine, nuciferin, dehydronciferine, anonoine, dehydrounonaine, N-methylisocoulaurine, prouciferine, N-nornuciferine, Ni-methyloclaurinc, oxoushinsunine, armepavine, N-norarmepavin, asimilobine, lirindine liensinine, isoleinsinine, neterine and nelumnine and β-sitosterol, glucose, pemitic acid and 10–monoacosanol.

Pharmacology

The juice of its tender leaves mixed with sugar is given in elephantiasis. Powdered rhizomes are prescribed for piles as demulcent and beneficial also in dysentery and chronic dyspepsia. The rhizome extract possesses antipyretic activity also. The flowers are cooling and astringent and are used in cholera, diarrhoea, fever and liver disease and their decoction is used as cardiac tonic.

Yuva (*Hordeum vulgare*)

तमूर्दरं न पृणतायवेनेन्द्रं सोमेभिस्तदपो वो अस्तु ।

अस्मभ्यं तहृसो दानाय राधः समर्थयस्व बहु तें वसव्यम् ॥

RV; 1.23.15

Description

It is an annual erect, stout and tufted grass about 5-12 m height. Leaves are few and linear–lanceolate, upper one close to the spikes; sheath is striate and ligules short and membranous. The spikes are terminal, linear–oblong, compressed, 5-6 cm long and densely flowered. The spikelets are sessile and arranged on two sides of a flattened rachis; all fertile or lateral ones barren and sometimes rudimentary. The glumes are 2, small, narrow, short–awned and enclosing three spikelets, lemma lanceolate and lodicules 2. The fruit is a caryopsis and elliptic, 9.0 cm long, short pointed, smooth free or adherent to palea or both to lemma and palea and groove on the inner face.

Phytochemistry

The seeds contain ubiquinones, proanthocyanidins, and chrysoeril. The barky grits contain pangamic acid. The stem and leaves contains flavones and cyaogenic glucoside besides, glycosides of horatines A and B are found in seeding.

Parts Used

The grains are used.

Pharmacology

The grains are demulcent and easy to digest and are used in the dietary. An ethyl alcohol (50 per cent) extract of the plant is antiprotozol and antiviral. The sutter, powder of the parched grain is much employed in the form of a gruel in case of painful and aortic dyspepsia, the sattu is also given to reduce sugar level in urine to diabetic patients. The ashes of the stalks are used for indigestion.

Vibhitaka (*Terminalia arjuna*)

प्रातर्यावाण रथ्येव वीराजेव यमा वरमा सचेथे ।

मेने इव तन्वा३ शुम्भमाने दम्पतीव तुविदा जनेपु ॥

RV; 10.34.1

Description

It is a large tree often with buttressed trunk, smooth grey bark and drooping branchlets about 20–25 m high. The leaves are usually sub-opposite, oblong of elliptic-long, pale dull green above and pale-brown beneath, 10.0–20.0 cm long and hard. The flowers are yellowish-white and are borne in shortly panicled-spikes. The fruits are 2.5–5.0 cm long drupes, ovoid or obovoid-oblong, fibrous woody, glabrous and with 5–7 equal, hard, coriaceaus and thick narrow wings.

Phytochemistry

The fruits contain alicylic and amino acids an polyols, arachidic, stearate, cerasidin, hentriacontane, myristyl oleacte, mannitol, β-sitoserol, friedelin, methyl oleanolute, ellagic and gallic acids, arjunic acid arjunone and tannin. The root bark yields arjunic acid, 2, 3, 23–trihydroxyl–olean-12 en–28-oic acid, arjunolic acid and its saponin, arjunoside I, II, III, and IV and 8 hydroxyhexadecanoic acid.

Pharmacology

The fruits are used as tonic and deobstruent. Externally, the leaves are used as a cover on sores and ulcers and their juice is used in earache. The bark is antidysenteric, antipyretic astiringent, cardiotonic, lithotriptic, stypmptomatic hypertension. A decoction of the thick bark made with milk is given every morning on an empty stomach or its powder with milk gur as a cardio tonic.

Khira (*Cucumis sativus*)

ॐ त्र्यम्बकंयजामहे सुगन्धिंम् पुष्टिवर्धनम् ।
उर्वारुकमिव बन्धनान मृत्योर्मुक्षीय मामृ तात् ॥

RV; 10.10.5-6

Description

It is slender and densely hespid annual herb. The leaves are large, simple, alternate, ovate-suborbicular, deeply cordate at base and 3-4 lobed. Flowers are large, yellow and monoecious. Male flowers are large, yellow and monoecious. Male flowers are clustered, bearing, anthers cohering, connective, crusted or above the cells. Female flower are solitary and cohered with bulbous–based haris. The fruits are large grayish–yellow hairs. The fruits are larger grayish–yellow or grayish—white and 10.0-25.0 cm × 2.5–3.7 cm seeds are many accuminate at both ends, white and smooth.

Phytochemistry

The fruits contain an enzyme erepsin, proteolytic enzyme, ascorbic acid oxidase, succinic and malic dehydrogenases.

Pharmacology

The fruits are sweet, refrigerant, haemostatic, tonic and diuretic. These are useful in hyperdipsia, burning sensation, thermoplegia, fever, insomnia, cephalagia, bronchitis, jaundice, hemorrhages, strangury and general debility.

The seeds are astringent, sweet, refrigerant, nutritive, purgative, antipyretic, tonic and diuretic and are used in burning sensation, constipation, intermittent fevers, streengury, renal calculus, urodynia and general debility.

Simpsapa (*Dalbergia sissoo*)

स्वप्नेननाभ्युप्या चुमुरिधुनि च जघन्थ दस्युं प्र दभीतिमाव: ।
रम्भी चिदत्र विविदे हिरण्यं सोमस्य ता मद इन्द्रैंकार ।।

RV; 7.50.3

Description

It is fairly large deciduous tree with grey bark up to 15-18m in height. The branches are downy, grey and spreading. The leaves are 3-5, alternate, imparimate, bifarious, roundish, accuminate and 3.5-6.0 cm × 3.0–5.4 cm. The flowers are sessile in axillary panicles shorter than leaves and yellowish white. The pod are 3.5–4.5 cm long, 1–4, kindney shapped and flat.

Phytochemistry

Leaves contain flavone and sissotin. The flower yield 7, 4-di-methyltectorigenin isolated mesoinositol 7-methyltectorigen in and a new flavone glycoside from the immature pods. While reported isocaviunin, tectorigenin, dalbergin, biochanin-A and 7-hydroxy-4 methylocoumarin, from the mature pods. The heart wood contains dalbergin, oMe-dalbergenone, hydroxyl and oMe-dalbergenones, dalbergichromene, nordalbergine, isodalbergin, allyphenal of latifolin, dalbergiphenol, OH-terans-stilbene and biochanin-A.

Pharmacology

The leaves are considered bitter and stimulant and their decoction is used in gonorrhoea. The bark is alterative and dried bark is haemostatic and is effective in bleeding piles, menorrhoea and in varicose veins. The wood is alterative and is used in leprosy, boils and eruption and to alloy vomiting. The roots are considered astringent. The plant is also used in Unani-system of medicine. The drug in Unani called, Shishan, Katel, is used as counter-irritant, anrisyphitic and blood purifier. The mucilage of the leaves mixed with sweet oil is used in exeoriation.

Salmali (*Bombax ceiba*)

यच्छल्मलौ भवति यन्नदीषु यदोषधीभ्यः परि जायते विषम् ।
विदेवा निरितस्तत्सुवन्तु मा मां पद्येन रपसा विदत्त्सरुः ॥

RV; 10.85.20

Description

The plant is a large handsome and deciduous are large spreading, glabrous and deciduous leaflets are 5-7, lanceolate, acuminate, tapering below, 15.0-20 cm long and quitentire, petioles are longer than leaflets. The flowers are crimson coloured, axillary or subterminal, usually solitary of clustered and appearing before the leaves. Fruits are 5-valved capsules, valved are woody and 10.0-12.0 cm long seed are many, globose and pale black. Flowering is during spring and winter season.

Phytochemistry

Bose and Dutta, isolated L-arabinose, D-galactose, D-galcturonic acid and rhabinose traces from the gum. The partial hydrolysis yields aldobiuronic acid. Bose and Dutta, further isolated 2, 4, 6, and 2, 3, 4-tri, 2, 6-di-o-methyl-D-galactose and 2, 3, 4-tri-o-methyl-D-galacturonic acid from the hydrolysis of the gum. β-sitosterol and its glucoside are found in all parts of the plant. The root yields triacontanol and a new glycoside. Fresh petals of the flower have essential oil, hentriacontriacontanal, quercetin, β-sitosterol and its glucosides, kaempferol, glucosides of pelaryonidin and cyaniding, 3-biosides and flavones.

Pharmacology

Prtused flower, leaves, root, bark, seeds and young fruits are the parts used. The flower are astringent and cooling. The paste of flower and leaves is applied in cutaneous diseases. Besides this, the leaves are also used as anti-inflammatory. The bark of stem is demulcent, emetic, styotic and tonic and its aqueous extract with the cured is used is to arrest blood-dysentery. The paste of the bark is used externally in cutaneous it is also used in gonorrhoea and syphilis, tuberculosis and in influenza. The young fruits are considered expectorant, stimulant and diuretic. These are useful in calculous affection, chronic inflammation and ulceration of kidneys and bladder.

Karsmarya (*Gmelina arborea*)

यज्ञायज्ञा वो अग्नये गिरागिरा च दक्षसे ।
प्रप्र वयमम त जातवेदस प्रिय मित्रं न शैसिषम् ॥

RV; 6.48.1-7

Description

It is an unarmed large deciduous tree about 20m high and pubescent with some white corky bark. The leaves are large, tawny tomentose. Underneath when young, cordate, ovate, accuminate and 10.0–20.0 × 7.5 -15.0 cm. The flowers are yellow tinged with browning terminal and axillary recemiform cymes. Inflorescence, calyx and corolla are toothed with dense soft and tawny tomentum. Fruits are ovoid of pyriform, smooth and 1.7–2.5 cm long drupex and orange–yellow when ripe. The seeds are oblong. Flowering is during February–April and fruiting April–July.

Phytochemistry

Arachidic, lauric, linoleic, myristic, oleic, palmitic and

stearic acids are found in seed oil. The leaves contain β–sitosterol, apigenin, lutelin and quercetin. The heartwood contains β–sitosterol, ceryl alcohol, gonelinol, arborone arbonreol, 1-hydroxy–2–methyoxy–2, gmelanone, gmelofuran, 2–piperonyl–3-hydroxy methyl–1-4-4–hydroxyl-1 tetrahydrofuran, gummadiol, arbinose, galactose, glucose, rhamnose and xylose. The root contain β–sitosterol, umbelloferone, benzoic acid, and octacosanal.

Pharmacology

The fruits are refrigerant and their decoction is given in fever and bilious affections. The leaves are demulcent and their juice is useful in cough gonorrhoea, foetid discharge and maggot in ulcers.

The pastes of the leaves are applied on head forelieve headache. The roots are bitter, tonic, demulcent, laxative, refrigerant and stomaching and their decoction is given inanasaco fever and indigestion.

Haridra (HALDI)

शुकेषु मे हरिमाणं रोपणाकासु दध्मसि ।
अथो हारिद्रवेषु मे हरिमाणं नि दध्मसि ।।

Description

The plant is a perennial herb about 90-120 cm tall with short stem and tufted leaves. Primary tubers are at the base of aerial stem and are ellipsoidal and bearing many rhizomes. The rhizomes have distinct taste. Root are fleshy with ellipsoidal tubers. The leaves are 25-40 cm × 10-15 cm linear, acuminate, ascending and pubescent beneath. The inflorescence is produced on short leaflets peduncles, consists of cone-shaped collection of numerous ovate bracts and an about 10-18 cm long and 5 cm broad. The flowers are pale-yellow and are borne in pairs in the axils. The seeds are black and shining with large, lace rate and white aril.

Phytochemistry

The rhizomes contain curccumin, zingiberine, p-rolynethyl carbinol and curcuminoids.

Pharmacology

The rhizomes and leaves are used. The rhizomes are aromatic, stimulant, carminative, and alterative, blood purifier, antiperiodic and tonic. Externally, those are applied to sprain and on wounds. Fresh juice often rhizome considered anthelmintic and is used as antiparastic in many skin affections. Its decoction is used on ingredient for stomachic preparations.

References

Arvindo, S. *On the Veda*. Printed at Shri Arvindo Ashram Press, Pondicherry, India.

Divedi, K.D., 1999. *A Cultural Study of Atharvaveda*. Vishvabharti Research Institute, Gyanpur (Badhoi, U.P., India).

Iyengar, S.P., 1983. *Righved Samhita*. The Soumya Press, Madras.

Kaushik, P. and Dhiman, A., 2000. *Medicinal Plants and Raw Drugs of India*. Bishan Singh and Mahendra Pal Singh, Dehradhun.

Nath, N., 1965. *Age of Rigveda*. Pharma K.L. Mukhopadhyay, Kolkata.

Priyavarat, S., 2003. *Dravyagun Vigyan*, Chokhamba Bharatiya Acadamy, Varanasi Vol. 2.

Shashtri, S.S.P. *Vidyalankar: Righved Samhita*. Veda Pratishthana, New Delhi.

Shastri, P.S., 1988. *Rigveda of Aesthetics*. Vidya Prakashan, New Delhi, India.

Srivastava, S.K. and J. Vidhyalankar, 1988. *Classical writings on vedic and Sanskrit Literature.* Dr. Virendra Arora on behalf of Swami Sradhanand Anusandhan Parkashan Kendra and Printed by New Educationals, Shahadra, Delhi.

Chapter 12

The Properties of Samidha and Samagri Used in Agnihotra

Navneet[1], D.R. Khanna[2], Shri Krishna[1] and Prabhat[1]

[1]Department of Botany & Microbiology,
[2]Department of Environmental Science,
Gurukul Kangri Vishwavidyalaya, Hardwar

Introduction

Agnihotra is the smallest form of Video Yajna, The Agnihotra is the traditional ritual to be performed daily by a householder in the morning after sunrise and in the evening before sunset. All religions have stressed on the need to purify the mind. The passions of the mind have a wonderful and powerful influence upon the state of the body and its disorders. The studies have documented that the purity of mind plays an important role in the control and care of many diseases. In our country people have a belief towards Agnihotra either by birth or by conviction. They have in their heart some feeling that by performing Agnihotra, regularly and faithfully, a new dimension in life is to be added. Agnihotra is an experience and once you have gone through its experience then rejection would not be possible for him. Agnihotra has never been a simple religious ritual, but has any minute scientific foundation based on fundamental principles. The implications of Agnihotra were forgotten during the early days or glamour of scientific achievements but are now perfomed almost in every country all over the world. While performing the Agnihotra an individual is expected to keep the place of the ritual clean. It therfore, becomes a habit for himself. In such a clean place, the Agnihotra makes the environment further pure and fully energised. This energy is both cosmic Pramatama Shakti and personal Jivatma Shakti. Thus, he builds up a mode of living or way of life which creates for himself and all his kith and kin a healthy environment. All of them enjoy a real peace of mind.

The materials required to perform the Agnihotra are samidha, Samagri, cowghee, havan kund, utensils and water. The properties of samidha *i.e.* fuel or wood sticks used for Agnihotra and the samagri *i.e.* herbal mixture used in Agnihotra are described in this article.

Samidha (Fuel or Wood Sticks for Yajna)

The wood which is used as a fuel for blazing the fire at the time of performing yajna is known as samidha. The samidha is thus collected from certain specific plants such as mango, pine, palasa, chandan, gular, khair, peepa, deodar etc. The fuelwood should be neat clean drying free from insects. It is about 12 to 15 cm in length and 3 cm in diameter. The first three samidhas are dipped in ghee and put in the yajna after litting the fire along with enchanting of mantras. If possible these samidhas are of chandan. If chandan is not available it should be of palasa, shami, gular, mango, bilva etc.

The nature of samidha as mentioned in our ancient literature should be taken into account. In 'Shatpath it is written as "तेजो हवा एतद्वनस्पतीनां यद् बाह्म शकलः" it means that the bark of tree is its strength and the specific property of samidha lies in its bark. Thus in Aahinksutra wali the samidha without bark is prohibited "विनिर्मुक्तत्वचा चैव" The wood sticks with bark is more beneficial and the properties of different wood sticks are given below:

आर्की नाशयंते व्याधि पलाशी सर्वकागदा।
खादिरी त्वर्थलाभायापामार्गी चेष्टवधिनी।
प्रजालाभाय चाश्वत्थी स्वर्गायोदुम्बरी भवेत्।
शमी शभयते पापं दूर्वा दीर्घायुरेव च।
कुशाः सर्वार्थकामाना परमं रक्षणं विदुः।।

(Vashistha Yajnapaditi)

Wood sticks of aok is effective in warding off diseases. Palasa is recommended for fulfilment of wishes. Khadir is used to get peace & prosperity. Shami is used for unseen problems and durva for longivity of life.

Aam (*Mangifera indica* Linn.)

This tree is indigenous to India and cultivated in many varieties almost every where in the plains and gardens. It is commonly known in Hindi as am and in English as mango and in Sanskrit as amva. It belongs to family anacardiaceae.

Pharmacology

The bark is astringent and is used in uterine haemorrhage, haemoptysis and haemorrhagic diarrhoea. The gum resin obtained from the stem is astringent and antisyphilitic.

Chandan (*Santalum album* Linn.)

This small tree is generally met with in the forests of southern India. The trees growing on hard, rocky, ferruginous soils are richer in oil than those growing on fertile tracts. It is commonly known in Hindi as Dak in English as white sandal wood tree and in Sanskrit as srigandha or chandanam. It belongs to family santalaceae.

Phytochemistry

Heart wood formation is accompanied by a large deposition of alcohol soluble constituents resins and the essential oil. The heart wood contains a volatile oil, a dark resin and tannic acid.

Pharmacology

Wood is bitter, cooling, sedative and astringent. Oil is astringent and disinfectant to the mucous membranes of geneto-urinary and bronchial tracts also diuretic expectorant and stimulant.

Gular (*Ficus glomerata* Roxb.)

It is a large tree found in all over India. It is commonly known in Hindi as gular and in English as clustor fig. It belongs to family urticaceae.

Phytochemistry

Bark contain tannin, wax and caoutchcuc and whole plant ash cantaining silica and phosphoric acid.

Pharmacology

Bark, leaves and unripe fruit are astringent, carminative stomachic and vermicide. A bath made of the fruit and bark is regarded as a cure for leprosy. Bank is used in the form of fine powder in dysentery, it is also applicable on conceraus affections.

Pipal (*Ficus religiosa* Linn.)

It is a large tree found wild as well as cultivated all over India. It is commonly known in Hindi as pipal and in English as peepal tree or sacred fig and in Sanskrit as propala. It belongs to family moraceae.

Phytochemistry

Bark contains tannin caoutchoue (cochtone) and wax.

Pharmacology

Bark is useful in gonorrhoea, ulcers and scabies in decoction with a little honey. Pulverised bark is used also in the heat of the blood. Bark is cooling astringent and sweet.

The bark is cooling, astringent and sweet The infusion or decoction or bark with honey in useful in gonorrhoea, ulcers and scabies. Pulverised bark is also used in the heat of blood (Rakta Daba).

Palasa (*Butea frondosa* Roxb.)

It is commonly known in Hindi as palas or tesu in English as bastard teak. It is commonly known as the "flame of the forest". It belongs to family papilionaceae.

Phytochemistry

Gum and bark contain kinotannic and gallic acids.

Pharmacology

Bark is useful in diarrhoea and dysentery and are used to disperse boils, pimoles and piles. Bark is given with ginger in snake bites. The gum is astringent.

Apamarg (*Achyranthes aspera* Linn.)

It is a small herb found in all over India. It is commonly known in Hindi as latjira, English as rough chaff tree and in Sanskrit as apamarg. It belongs to family amaranthaceae.

Phytochemistry

The plant contains betaine, water soluble alkaloid phyranthine, oleanolic acid, glucose, galactose, rhamnose, xylose, vitamins, amino acids, nitrogen and protein.

Pharmacology

The plant possesses valuable medicinal properties as pungent and laxative and is considered useful in dropsy, piles, boils, eruptrons of the skin etc. The decoction of the plant is useful in pneumonia, cough and kidney stones, diuretic and efficaceaus in renal dropsies.

Khadira (*Acacia catechu* Linn.)

It is common in forests of India and Burma. It belongs to family Mimosaceae. It is commonly called in Sanskrit as Khadira, in English as Black catechu and in Hindi as Khair.

Phytochemistry

The wood contains catechu tannic acid, catechuic acid or catechin, catechu red tannin, gum quercetin.

Pharmacology

The bark is bitter and acrid, cooling astringent to the bowels anthelmintic antidysenteric, antipyretic, curesitching, sore throat bronchitis, indigestion ulcers, boils, urinary discharges, strengthens the teeth (Nadakarni, 1976).

Yajna Samagri

The important part of Vedic yajna is the samagri used in performing the yajna. The ingredients used in the yajna samagri have medicinal properties at the core of them. These properties get spread in the atmosphere after the performance of yajna and exact, synchronize the circadian corresponding to sunrise and sunset. This results in beneficial effects on the body, mind and wisdom of the persons performing the yajna. An atmosphere of tranquillity, genial understanding and discipline develops. The atmosphere is filled with healthy nutrients and its fragrance pleases the mind. Moreover, the ingredients present inside the samagri plays an important role in controlling microbial population in the atmosphere. Thus the effect of yajna samagri on survival of saprophytic and pathogenic microbes in the atmosphere helps in treating air borne infections.

Methods of preparation of Yajna Samagri

The following points are taken into consideration at the time of preparation of yajna samagri:

1. The ingredients should be collected separately and kept to different labeled polythene bags. The ingredients must be authentic and pure. The old and rotten ingredients should not be used.

2. The fresh and green medicinal plants (*e.g. Tinospora cordifolia* etc.) are to be used in yajna samagri after cutting them into pieces and drying in the sunlight for one or two days.
3. The ingredients should be cut into small pieces and are to be mixed properly.
4. *Cinnamomum camphora* (Kapur), *Crocus sativas* (Kesar), *Myristica fragrans* (javatri), sugar and ghee will be kept separately and are to be used as follows:
   (*a*) *Cinnamomum camphora* is to be used for the lightening of fire.
   (*b*) *Crocus sativas* and *Myristica fragrans* are to mixed in ghee.
   (*c*) As per the requirements of the yajna samagri, sugar, kapur, honey etc. should be mixed.
   (*d*) Pure ghee is to be added in sufficient quantity so that the yajna samagri does not give a dry appearance.
5. Cow's ghee is the most important and essential ingredient prescribed in the performance of yajna as ordained by the vedas. In case it is not available then buffalow's ghee can be used but refined vanaspati ghee for performing yajna is highly improper and harmful.

The yajna samagri for different seasons is given in Tables 8.1 to 8.6 (Agnihotri, 1995 and Chunekar, 1969).

Shatavar (*Asparagus racemosus*)

It is a much branched perennial herb. It is found in tropical and subtropical India. It is commonly known as

Shatavar and in Sanskrit as Atirasa, Shatamuli, Shatavar, It belongs to family Liliaceae.

Description

The flowers are white, fruits are red or redish violet. Flowering is in Oct.-Nov. and fruiting during cold season.

Phytochemistry

The plant contains fruits and flowers yield rutin, hyeroside, querecetin, orsitosterol and furostanolic saponins.

Pharmocology

Roots and bark of the shatavar generally used in fever, rheumatism and also useful in piles. The bark is antibacterial and antifungal.

Sarson (*Brassica campestris*)

It is a glaucous annual herb. It is cultivated throughout India. It is commonly known as sarson, in English as mustard Indian Sanskrit as sarshapa. It belongs to family Cruciferae.

Description

The flowers are yellow coloured. Flowering & fruiting during January-March.

Phytochemistry

The seed oils contains glycerides of palmitic, linotenic, erucic acids. Neutral sugar analysis of polysaccharides of seed epidermis yield arbinose, glucose, mannose and galactose.

Pharmacology

The oil forms and efficaceous embrocation in muscular rheumatism and stiffneck. It is used in dengu fever. The roots and leaves are considered stomachic. The seed mixed with hot water used in irritant jaundice.

Piyal (*Buchanania lanzan*)

It is a moderate sized tree. It is commonly known as Piyal, in Sanskrit as Prigal and in English as Almond tree. The plant is found in hot and drier parts of India. It belongs to family Anacardiaceae.

Description

The flowers are small, bisexual, crowded and greenish white. The fruits are globose, compressed and black drupes with hard stones. Flowering is in Jan-March and fruiting during March-May.

Phytochemistry

The seeds contains linolein amino acids and stericacids. The leaves yield gallotannins. The bark contains saponin, reducing sugars and alkaloids.

Pharmacology

The leaves powder used in wounds. Exudate gum from the stem is used in intercostal pains. The seeds are used as antidiarrhoeal.

The fruits are used in tonic or in prickly heat, itch and pimples. Root possess anticancer activity.

Dhak (*Butea monosperma*)

It is a moderated size deciduous tree. It is commonly known in Hindi as Dhak, in English as flame of the forest and in Sanskrit as palasha. It belongs to family Papilionaceae.

Description

The bark is fibrous, bluish grey or light brown and exuding a ruby red vitreous gum. Flowering in Feb.-March and fruiting during April-May.

Phytochemistry

The flowers contain butin. The gum from bark contains riboflavinthimin. Seeds contain palasonin.

Pharmacology

The seeds are used in flatulence and piles. The flowers are given in leucorrhoea and their juice is given to induce sterility in women. Bark used in tumours, bleeding piles and ulcers. Leaves in pimples, tumours, hemorrhage.

The juice of leaf is used in skin diseases. The roots used in elephentiasis.

Brahmi (*Centelia asiatica*)

It is a prostrate perennial herb. It is commonly known in Hindi as Brahmi, in Sanskrit as Brahmi, mundikparni. It belongs to family Umbelliferae.

Description

The flowers are purple white. Flowering is in July-August, fruiting later on during October-December.

Phytochemistry

The plant contains an alkaloid, brahmine, steroids, bacogenin A of three types.

Pharmacology

The whole plant is used. The juice of leaves is given in fever, also useful in a cataract and other eye problems.

Kapur (*Cinnamomum camphora*)

It is a tail evergreen tree. It is in Hindi called Kapur, in English Camphor and in Sanskrit Chandra. It belongs to family Lauraceae.

Description

The bark is aromatic, rough from outside and smooth inside. Wood is yellowish-brown, flowering is in March-April and fruitng in July-August.

Phytochemistry

The plant contains camphor.

Pharmacology

The camphor is used in insecticidal preparations. The vapours of camphor are inhaled in cold and affections of chest or with olive oil used externally in muscular strains, rheumatism and inflammations.

Dub (*Cynodon dactylon*)

It is a perennial herb. It is commonly known in Hindi as Hariall dub, in Sanskrit as Durva and in English as Conch. It belongs to the family Graminae.

Description

Flowering is during July-September and fruiting in October.

Phytochemistry

Information not available.

Pharmacology

Whole plant in the form of panchang is used. Also in dropsy and in secondary syphillis, chronic diarrhoea and dysentry.

Nagarmotha (*Cyperus rotundus*)

It is a perennial glabrous herb. It is commonly known in Hindi as Moth, in Sanskrit as Mustak. It belongs to family Cyperaceae.

Description

The flowers are reddish brown. The plant occurs throughout India. Flowering and fruiting is during July-December.

Phytochemistry

The tubers contain essential oil.

Pharmacology

The tubers are used in disorder of the stomach and irritation of the bowels. The root paste is used in healing wounds, and eye disease.

Lajwanti (*Mimosa pudica*)

It is diffuse or spreading under shrub. It is commonly known in Hindi as Lajwanti, in English as Sensitive plant and in Sanskrit as Lajjalu. It belongs to the family Mimosaceae.

Description

The flowers are as soft as cotton in pinkish globose heads. Flowering is during August-September, fruiting in November-December. It is a native of tropical America and subtropical parts of India.

Phytochemistry

The plant contains mimosine, crocetin dimethyl ester and tannin.

Pharmacology

The leaves of the plant are used in sinus sores, piles and fistula. The decoction of the roots is useful in gravel and other urinary complains. Their paste is used in glandular swellings.

Kaunch (*Mucuna pruriens*)

It is an annual herbaceous twiner. It is commonly known as Kaunch, in English as Cowhage and in Sanskrit as Kapikacchu. It belongs to family Papilionaceae.

Description

The flowers are dark violet flowering during September-October and fruiting in December-March.

Phytochemistry

The seed oil contain palmitic, oleic and stearic acids.

Pharmacology

The pods are anthelminthic. The seeds are a prodisian and nervine tonic and used in scorpion stings. The roots is beneficial in urinary problems and delirium in fevers. Roots given in Cholera with honey. An ointent in oil is used for elephantosis.

Kamal (*Nelumbo nucifera*)

It is commonly known in Hindi as Kamal, in English as Indian Lotus, sacred lotus and in Sanskrit as Padama. It belongs to the family Nympheaceae.

Description

It is an attractive perennial herb. Flowers are yellow. Flowering during summer-autumn and fruiting is winter season.

Phytochemistry

The plants contains a number of alkaloids.

Pharmacology

The juice of its tender leaves mixed with sugar is given in Elephentiosis. Powdered rhizomes in piles, chronic dyspepsia. The flowers are considered also as antidote to poisons.

Tulsi (*Ocimum sanctum*)

It is commonly known in Hindi as Tulsi, in Sanskrit as Sursa and in English as Basil. It belongs to family Labiatae.

Description

It is an errect and much branched herb. The stem and branches are clothed with soft hairs. Flowering and fruiting is during almost throughout the year. It is cultivated throughout India.

Phytochemistry

The essential oils from leaves and flowering tops yields phenols.

Pharmacology

The plant is considered expectorant, stomachic, diuretic, antiseptic and cardiac stimulant. The root decoction is given in Malarial fevers. The flowers with honey, ginger and onion juice are used in cough as expectorant.

Chaavl (*Oryza sativa* Linn.)

It is commonly known in Hindi as Chaavl, Dhan, in Sanskrit as Dhanya and in English as Rice. It belongs to family Gramineae.

Description

It is an annual grass with erect culms and glabrous nodes. Leaves are accuminate, scabrid on the upper surface and along the margin and glabrous on the lower surface. The plant is sown as a crop during June-July and ripens during winter. It is widely cultivated as a crop plant throughout India.

Phytochemistry

Silver skin contains oryzanin and bran contain a glucoside nukain which on hydrolyis yield aglucane nukagenin. The grains contain protein, fat, carbohydrate, ascorbic acid, thiamine, riboflavin, nicotinic acid, pyrodoxine, vitamin A, calcium, magnesium, sodium. phos phorous, iron and copper.

Pharmacology

Rice gruel is given in disorganized digestion, in bowel complaints, dysentry and diarrhoea. It is also useful in gastric ulcer, smallpox, measles, scarlet fever, gonorrhoea. Rice flower is dusted thickly over the surface forms a very cooling and soothing application in smallpox, measles, erysipelas, prickly heat and other inflammatory skin infections and also to burns and scalds. Rice poultice used like linseed meal poultice.

Khajur (*Phoenix saylvestre*)

It is commonly known in Hindi as Khajur, in Sanskrit as Kharjur and in English as wild date palm. It belongs to the family Arecaceae.

Description

It is a tall and errect palm tree reaching a height upto 18 m with thick hemispherical crown. The fruit is oblong ellipsoid, orange yellow to reddish brown and edible berry. Seeds are rounded at ends, grooved to centre on one face pale brown and about 1.6 cm long. Flowering in summer and fruiting later during September-October. It is tolerably common throughout India, wild or more often cultivated.

Phytochemistry

The sap from the trunk of the plant called Nira is a good source of ascorbic acid, protein, sugar, phosphorous, calcium, iron, thiamine, riboflavin, nicotonic acid, tartaric acid. The fruits are said to have proteins, fat, carbohydrates, calcium and phosphorous.

Pharmacology

Fruits as tonic and restorative juice is used for beverage. The sap is used as slightly nacrotic and digestive. The root is used in toothache and in nervous debility. The plant is used in gonorrhoea and gleet.

Chir (*Pinus roxburghii*)

It is commonly known in Hindi as Chir, in Sanskrit as Sarala and in English as Chirpine. It belongs to the family Pinaceae.

Description

It is a large tree with symmetrical branches high upto the trunk and forming a round head of light foliage and reaches upto 30 m in height.

It is an evergreen but becomes completely or partiailly deciduous in dry season. The bark is dark grey and deeply fissured. The leaves are 20 cm long arranged in clusters of three finely toothed and light green. The cone formation is started in January next year during Jun-July. Its cones become old and in next summer burst and seeds are shed out. About 26 months are spared to complete the white process. The dry cones remain long on the tree. It is found in the Himalayas from Kashmir to Sikkim and in the Shivalik Hills.

Phytochemistry

The plant contains α and β pinene and β carene. The needles of the plants are good source of Vitamin C & E and carotenes. The heart-wood contains stibene and flavonoids.

Pharmacology

The wood is stimulant diaphoretic and is useful in the burning of the body, cough, fainting and ulceration, beneficial in snake bite and scorpion stings, gonorrhoea, used in chronic bronchitis. The oil from the wood is used in rheumatic pain. Its vapours releive the spasm of whooping cough and asthma, given in indigestion, loss of appetite and intestinal worms.

Safed Chandan (*Santalum album*)

It is commonly known in Hindi as Safed Chandan, in Sanskrit as Chandana, Srikhand and in English as Sandal tree. It belongs to family Santalaceae.

Description

It is a small evergreen, glaborous and semi parasitic tree with slender branches attaining a height upto 18m with dark grey or nearly black or reddish and rough bark, sapwood is unscented and white, but heart-wood is scented and yellowish brown or dark brown. The seeds are ovoid or globose. It is Round in Vindhya Mountains southward, particularly in Karnataka, Tamil Nadu, Rajasthan, Uttar Pradesh, Madhya Pradesh.

Phytochemistry

The leaves, fruits and seeds contain santalbic acid, oleic acid, linolic acid and glucose, β santalic acid, teresantalic, santanone from the sandal oil.

Pharmacology

The wood ground up with water into a paste is applied to the temples in headache, fevers and local inflammations and to skin diseases to alooy head and pruntus and also used as diaphoretic. A decoction of the wood mixed with that of dried ginger is used in hoemorrhoids. Oil is used for cooling, diuretic, diaphoretic and expectorant and used in dysciria, gonorrhoeal urethritis and cystitis or for pimples the plant is also used in Unani medicines as germicide, blood purifier, antiseptic and fungicide.

Amrita (*Tinospora cordifolia*)

In Hindi it is known as Amrita, Sanskrit as Gurnchi and English as Gulanchea tinospora. It belongs to family Menispermaceae.

Description

It is a large glabrous and climbing succulent shrub with rocky bark. The flowers are small, yellow and unisexual, male flowers are fascicled and females are usually solitary. The seeds are curved. Flowering is during summer and fruiting in winter. It is found in tropical India.

Phytochemistry

The plant contains tinosporin, columbin, chasmanthin, palmarin, berberine, giloin, palmatosides C and F from the stem of the plant.

Pharmacology

The leaves are prescribed in fevers the stem is bitter, stomachic and antipyretic, juice is given in jaundice and decoction is used for rheumatic fever and vomitting due to excessive secretion. A kind of starch, known as Gdoeka sat is prepared from the aqueous extract of dry stem which is used as tonic and antidysentric and antacid substance. The root is considered as powerful emetic and is used for visceral obstruction, also used in lever disorders.

Shambhalu (*Vitex negundo*)

It is commonly known in Hindi as Shambalu, in Sanskrit as Nirgundi and in English as five leaved chaste. It belongs to family Verbanaceae.

Description

It is a deciduous shrub with thin grey bark. The flowers are small and bluish purple and are born in lateral chymes forming an elongated terminal thyrses and often compounded the base. Flowering is during June-August and fruiting in cold season. It is found in scrub jungles and road side.

Phytochemistry

The seeds contains β-sitosterol, p-hydroxy benzoic and δ-hydroisopthalic acids, linoteic, palmitic, oleic acid. The leaves yields β-sitosterol glucomanitol, carotene, vitamin C. The root contains β-sitosterol, acetyl oleanlic acid, vaniolic acids and luteolin.

Pharmacology

The leaves are vermifuge arematic, lonic alternative anodyne, antiparasitic, discutient, antiinflammatory and antirheumatic. A smoke of dried leaves is taken headache and catarrh and dullness of hearing and also as both in the puerperal state of women. Juice is used in foetial discharges and worms in gonorrhoeal epididymitis and orchitis and also over sprained limbs contusions and leech bites. Roots used in boils, colic dyspepsia, leprosy, piles, dysentry. Plant is used in asthma, bronchitis, consumption, eye diseases, leucoderma and painful leething.

Angur (*Vitis vinifera*)

It is commonly known in Hindi as Angur, in Sanskrit as Drakona and in English as Grape. It belongs to family Vitaceae.

Description

It is a large woody climber with bifid tendrils. The leaves are glabours, clothed beneath with grey deciduous to mentum suborbicular cordate. The flowers are pentamerous and green and are borne in ombel like cymes. Fruits come to perfection due to heavy rainfall. Flowering is during April-May. Fruiting in June-July and found in West Asia and in North West regions.

Phytochemistry

The mature fruits contain malic tartaric acid, recemic, oxalic acid.

Pharmacology

The grapes are used in chronic bronchitis, heart-diseases. Bright disease and gout. The juice of the unripe grapes used in affections, contipating in teething, leaves used in diarrohoea. Dried fruits known as munakka are used in fevers, heat of body, cough, hoarseness, consumption and in wasting diseases. Ashes of the wood used in stone, cold swelling of the testes and in piles.

Ashwagandha (*Withania somnifera*)

It is commonly known in Hindi as Ashgandh and in Sanskrit as Aswagandha. It belongs to family Solanaceae.

Description

It is an erect and much branched perennial undershrub, flowering is in July-August, fruiting during January-February.

Phytochemistry

The leaves contain withanone, many withanolides, somnirol, somnitol, alkaloids and withaferins. The root possesses anhggrine, withsomimin and C-28 steriod lactones.

Pharmacology

Fruits used in chest comoplaints. The seeds are hypatonic and diuretic and are used in chest complaints and congulating milk. The seeds are hypnotic and diunetic. The leaves are antipyretic, antihelmintic and bitter. The bruised leaves are applied in carbuncles scobies, ulcers and painful swellings and a fomentation of its leaves is used for sore eyes and swollen hands and test. The root is used in cough, dropsy, leucorrhoea, cough, menstrual problems, to restore loss of memory in nervous exhaustion, spermatorrhoea and seminal debility. A decoction of the root is used with long pepper, ghee and honey in scrotula and the uterus of women who is habitual of miscarriage.

Kurchi (*Holarrhena adysenterica*)

It is a small decidous tree. It is commonly known in Hindi as Indrajau, Kurch, in Sanskrit as Kutaja and in English as Conessi.

Description

The flowers are white and slightly scanted. Flowering is during April-July and fruiting from August-October. It is found in tropical parts of India.

Phytochemistry

The leaves contain holantooines A, B, E and F. The stem bark contains hoarrhenine, Kurchleine.

Pharmacology

The bark is used in dysentry and is rubbed over the body in dropsy. The seeds are used bleeding piles, chronic chest affection asthma and in colic pain. The leaves are used in chronic bronchitis and also applied to boils and ulcers. The roots are given to cattle in disease in which tongue ejects out and get swollen.

References

Agnihotri, F.L. 1949. *Yajya Chikitsa*, Seth Ratansi Heerji Yajya Chikitsa Sanatorium, Jablapur,

Agnihotri, F.L. 1995, *Dev Yajya*. Vedic Pustakalaya Dayanand Ashram, Ajmer.

Chunekar, K.C. 1969. *Bhavaprakash Nighantoo Commentry*. Chaukhamba Prakashan, Varanasi.

Joshi, K.L. 1999. *Atharvaveda Samhita*. Chaukamba Prakashan. Delhi.

Kaushik, P. and Dhiman, A.K. 2000. *Medicinal Plants and Raw Drugs of India*.

Navneet, S. Chand and Sharma, V.K. 1998, *Agnihotra-The Air Purifier*. Aryabhatt, Gurukul Kangri University, Vijana Patrika, 1: 83-86.

Narayan, K.P. 1987, *Agnihotra: Vedic Way to Beat Pollution.* Vedoddharini, XV: 60-63.

Potdar M.M. 1993. *Agnihotra.* Institute for studies in Vedic Science, Shivpuri, Akkalkot.

Saraswati, S.P. 1984. *Agnihotra: Daily Fire Ritual.* Dr. Ratna Kumari Svadhyay Sansthana, Allahabad.

Nadakarni, A.K. 1976. *Indian Materia Medica.* Bombay Popular Prakashan.

Index